BREXITPRENEURSHIP

RICHARD WOODS

Copyright © 2017 RICHARD WOODS
All rights reserved.
ISBN-13: 978-1981128501

CONTENTS

CHAPTER 1
WE ARE HERE

CHAPTER 2
WE ARE GOING HERE

CHAPTER 3
THIS IS HOW YOU WIN

RICHARD WOODS

DEDICATED TO

Cara, Mylo & Poppy

Praise For Brexitpreneurship

"Through the successful development of digital marketing agency, Yomp, Richard has helped support the growth of a vast range of businesses across a multitude of industry sectors nationwide.

Key to business development, Richard has experienced firsthand the ups and downs of the UK Business sector, but nothing has or will quite be like Brexit.

Although its full impact is yet to the be known, the warning signs are clear and for Business Owners, it is evident we are entering an uncertain and extremely challenging period.

That said, Richard is without a doubt one of the best people to be able to guide Entrepreneurs through Brexit, and through his invaluable commentary and advice within Brexitpreneurship, will ensure readers will feel empowered to come out on top - fighting."

Mark Wright - Winner of BBC's The Apprentice 2014 - Co-Founder of Climb Online – Business Partner of Lord Sugar

"Richard is an inspirational and indefatigable entrepreneur whom we've worked closely with for a few years on various projects.

His focused support for small local businesses balanced with his high profile national work, makes him the ideal spokesperson for leading British entrepreneurs through the challenges of thriving under the new reality of Brexit."

David and Jarmila Yu - Founders - YUnique Marketing Ltd

"Business is going to be effected in all sorts of ways, but there will also be plenty of opportunity. For my business, I can't predict what will happen. I am certain the labor force will be effected, I am sure overseas trade will get harder, but as a versatile business owner I will have to adapt to change.

The harder it will get the less competition I will have. Opportunity sometimes comes from the hardest of times, you just have to be read for it.

Until it happens, the best thing I can do is to get on with focusing on what matters now, absorb the thought leadership of others such as Richard and this book and be ready for change."

John Gower - Founder - Omni Local

"Richard is certainly the modern day entrepreneur and an excellent marketer with a keen interest in business. He can regularly be found reading the business section of newspapers and on radio discussing all things business. I think it is down to entrepreneurs to fly the flag for the UK and focus on what we are good at."

Gary Das CeMAP - Founder - Active Brokers

"Many feel that leadership is about the management of change and Brexit has the potential to create considerably change. Achieving sales targets will remain the lifeblood of an organisation and Richard has the expertise and charisma to support commercial leadership, providing mentoring and guidance to you and your team to help ensure your long term business ambition is achieved."

Colin Sales - Founder - 3C Consulting

"Today I sat down to read a few pages of 'Brexitpreneur' and finished it in one go: a most pleasant relaxing Sunday afternoon read over a few cups of tea (English Breakfast) that I have encountered in a long time.

It provided a critical, yet positive and forward thinking, analysis of the future for SMO's and Britain: better and younger than many I have read for some time throughout countless press reports and TV comments.

I feel much cheered and more positive for the whole future of British business after reading Richard Woods' latest business book – and I found myself googling a whole new range of products, innovations, schemes and businesses that I had never heard of.

It additionally introduced me to a whole new slant of responses to the challenge of our decade which rightly identified Generation Y as the best equipped to take up the exciting mantle of worldwide opportunity post Brexit."

SMW

Introduction

The era of the Brexitpreneur

It seemed unlikely, it seemed impossible... yet here we are.

On the 23rd June 2016, the UK voted to leave the EU and now the business community must power through and make the best of what was commonly considered to be a bad outcome for business and the economy.

I voted to remain and I was shocked when I heard the result.

When I began my current business, I considered the 6 years until 2020 my empire building years and a rocky, uncertain economy was the last thing I wanted.

It has however happened. The UK public has spoken and like any period of change, there will be winners and there will be losers.

The purpose of this book is to guide UK entrepreneurs through the pros and the cons of Brexit, and to give a clear methodology for taking the bull by the horns and succeeding in this era of uncertainty.

When setting out to write this book, I researched the definition of Entrepreneurship, which is a French-originated word, coined by the economist Jean-Baptiste.

I discovered it has the following meaning:

'taking charge of your own business'.

It is perhaps appropriate that the 'take charge' definition falls in line with some of the main headlines from the 'Leave' campaign during the vote.

It was therefore fitting that I coin a phrase for this new era and so the word 'Brexitpreneurship' was born.

Brexitpreneurship: *The art of organising and managing an enterprise through the period of the UK's exit from the EU and beyond.*

The modern Brexitpreneurs will be the business leaders who steady their ship and put the Great back in front of Britain once more.

We have seen but also overcome uncertain seas before.

I started my first business in 2007, just in time for the biggest global recession ever recorded. I had ups and downs, but I ultimately won through, and now like many other business owners I am steading myself and my businesses for this next adventure into the unknown.

Only the strongest will survive. Only the business owners with the right plan, the right mind-set and who understand that the old way is in fact just 'old', will win.

The dawn of the Brexitpreneur is here.

CHAPTER 1

WE ARE HERE

That Morning

On the 24th of June, 2016, I woke up in my European bed, rolled over, turned off my European alarm clock, and walked down the European stairs. I got changed, walked out of my European door into my European car.

I was nervous and excited...

...not because of the generation-defining news that was unfolding.

I had not even cast a thought to that, it was after all a foregone conclusion: we would never exit.

It was my brother's wedding day and I was the best man. I had penned a very rough speech which I hadn't properly prepared or even practiced.

Lost in my thoughts, I turned on my European radio and meandered towards the wedding venue. Out of nowhere my ears caught Peter Gordon talking on his Breakfast Show. He was talking to Bev about some big news that had happened. My mind was practicing the best man's speech over and over and it hadn't dawned on me that any of this news would be important. Until he made a joke.

The joke was, "Are we still allowed to play in the European Football Championship now we're not European?"

I laughed, because I thought he was being sarcastic. Little did I know at that time, how significant that comment was. I drifted back into rehearsing my speech. I continued along my European roads and I neared the wedding venue. It was my parents' house in the small Surrey village of Windlesham. There'd been a massive downpour of rain that day. Many of the wedding party were milling around, getting ready, brooms sweeping water off the marquee floor, pumps pumping out the water. It was all hands on deck. It was one of the biggest downpours of rain that Surrey had ever seen, and it happened the night before my brother's wedding.

As I pull into my parent's gate, Peter Gordon comments again about being out of Europe. "What?" Suddenly, my whole world became acutely focused on that news. I hadn't even cast a thought on it.

I'd been a Remainer; everybody I spoke to had been a Remainer. Every single person that I worked with, or friend I had discussed it with had been talking up Remain. There was a few people I knew; my father, and a few others, that were Leavers. But I just thought that they are the older generation. That's how they feel. But we would never ... Nobody would be silly enough to rock the boat.

I sat there in my car, dumbfounded.

Absolutely dumbfounded at the news. I turned the volume up, and it was right. I immediately got out my phone, headed onto the Telegraph website, and there it was in big letters, "BREXIT;

Britain has exited the EU".

We voted to leave.

I could not believe it. I was flabbergasted. 52% to 48%. With a 75% turn out. There was no argument. Millions of people had voted to leave the EU. It wasn't even on my radar. I voted the previous day, like many others. I had even laughed when one of my good friends, Daniel Priestly said:

"Figure this, the rain in London is going to stop many London voters voting, and we Brexit because of the weather,"

I had laughed. Maybe, maybe that wasn't such a silly thing to say? London after all was predominantly Remain.

I needed more information. I ran into my parent's house, flicked on the TV and just stood there. My mother came in to join me and we just stood and watched and watched. Shock. I was absolutely shocked. What does this mean for me? What does this mean for my business? What does it mean for my kids? What does this mean? I think that's probably the one phrase everybody had on their lips that morning.

Even now, as I write this book, that question keeps on coming to the fore: what does this mean? What does this mean for us? What has this meant and what will this mean in the future? Are we European anymore? Are we British? Are we going to be ostracised? Are we going to be cut off? Or are we going to become more global, more worldly? Is this just the start? Is Europe breaking apart?

What about the economy? What about a recession? We've just come out of the deepest, longest recession that we've ever known. Nobody's got the appetite for another recession. We are just on the recovery. We've got great economic forecasts, we were one of the fastest growing economies in Europe, highest growing net GDP at the end of 2015. And there my mother and I stood in silence, in the middle of 2016, watching the UK's public fundamentally rocking the carefully crafted ship that we were sailing.

What now?

Who am I?

My name is Richard Woods and I am a British entrepreneur.

Since graduating from university in 2006, I have joined forces with my brother Tim to build a number of great businesses by harnessing the power of technology and the internet.

At the date of publishing, we run a portfolio of companies and investments, including an award winning digital marketing agency, Yomp Marketing.

Looking back, it was clear that Tim and I learned the foundations of business growing up in an entrepreneurial household. Our father grew his oil business (also with his brother), starting with a small paraffin delivery job selling the bottles door-to-door (like a milkman, but with paraffin for house heaters), into the largest independent home heating oil distributer in the UK, with over 250 staff and turning over half a billion pounds per annum.

He was nominated for both the Entrepreneur of the Year and the City Deal of the Year awards within his 40 year career.

His story was a humble-beginning-to-riches story and it was impossible not to be inspired by his drive and talents. He would always push my brother, sister and me to take our own initiative and would make us work for everything.

When I asked him to cast his mind back to what *joining* the EU meant for businesses, he said that the vote was actually for whether we should join the Common Market. Prior to the Common Market trading with another European country was fraught with red tape and paperwork. The Common Market did away with all that: a single market with no trade barriers or customs duties.

My mother also had a big role in inspiring us as kids. She would regularly take us to museums and exhibitions, opening our minds to the world. On long drives she would play audio books in the car – not the usual children's audio books, but business audio books!

I learned how Alan Sugar built Amstrad, how Anita Roddick build The Body Shop and how Richard Branson built the Virgin empire.

They all taught me to dream and to stay hungry. Inspired by Branson, I still want to own my own Necker Island, and this is a massive driver of my personal ambition. It is my screen saver, it is on my wall, I even research it during my down time.

In education, I fine-tuned my learning when I proudly studied Business with Entrepreneurship at Southampton Solent University and received a first class honours for my final thesis 'Is there a link between Dyslexia and Entrepreneurship?'.

After graduating I set off to India and China at the age of 22, with a sketch book of idea, a small amount of funding and a graduate loan. I walked the trade show halls of Delhi, Hong Kong, Shenzhen and Guangzhou meeting potential suppliers and cutting my teeth in the world of international negotiation.

For the next 3 years I ran an international importation business, concentrated on the European gifts market.

At its height, we had a 4 sales agents in Ireland, and 3 in the UK plus a fully functioning distribution centre, shipping to all of Europe, but also to places such as the US, the Falkland Islands, Iceland and Sweden.

Our trade was based primarily upon independent high street gift shop owners who, when in 2007 the credit crunch hit, were some of the most affected. Typically these shops were fun little side projects for a couple, retirees or two friends, and when the going got tough most of my clients cut their losses and quickly closed.

We were left with a few struggling national stores, a slowing economy and bad debts everywhere.

So we had only one option: to diversify or die. I did the only thing I knew, and that was to try and help our client base as much as possible. Our concept was to give them so much support that our products would take prominence in their shop and therefore we would grow as they grew.

That support came in the way of regular visits and time spent with them helping to install new window displays, better on-shelf designs and layouts, and quickly moved into helping to create local events, such as a St George's day event on the high street, or an Easter sales event.

At the time, we had also built our own website www.funky-gifts.co.uk (now closed), for which we received regular compliments from our trade customers. They started asking who our web developer was. We had built it ourselves, and this triggered an idea for a potential opportunity.

We started offering a website to our customers for free, if they brought £1,000 worth of stock from us. This went down really well, but in 2 months' time when we went back for the re-order of the gifts, the customer would open up their stock room door and there would be stacked hundreds of our products, which due to the market conditions, were simply not selling. However, the customer would ask for more pages on their website, or would introduce us to their friend who was a plumber, who definitely did not want £1,000 worth of stock from us, but really liked the website we had built and needed one himself.

So we soon realised that there was great untapped opportunity for the type of websites we were building, and a real need for them in the struggling small business market during the credit crunch.

So in 2009 we officially pivoted away from importation and into website design and build.

Since then my brother and I have grown a portfolio of businesses all focusing on the internet and technology, employing 18 members of staff, producing a bestselling marketing book (Digital

TrailBlazer), an award-winning outsourced marketing department service (Digital TrailBlazer Done For You), founded and continue to run the UK's largest Lead Generation Conference (The Lead Gen Summit) and have the UK's first Lead Generation Academy.

I also feel honored to have been recognised as Young Entrepreneur of the Year 2016 (Haines Watts – Regional Winner jointly with my brother Tim), Key Person of Influence Award 2015 (Dent Global Annual Awards), and involved in Marketing Campaign of the Year 2015 (Inspire Business Awards).

I was also able to leverage this experience to beat a pool of 80,000 applicants to compete to become Lord Sugar's Apprentice on the BBC, Series 11 (2015), where I was a finalist and the top seller across all tasks, won 8 out of 10 tasks and broke two Apprentice records: One for most sales in one day (£4.3 million) and the other for "The Best Advertising Task ever seen on The Apprentice" – *Lord Sugar.*

I hope my story to date shows that even when my business was in its early years, to succeed I had to be reactive to the markets. When forces way outside your control change the face of your business landscape, you have to be prepared to innovate, change direction and fight to survive.

This is the position we all may find ourselves in, as business owners going through the unknown of Brexit and beyond.

Like the credit crunch, these are uncharted seas, and there will be casualties, and there will be jobs and fortunes lost.

But as my father always told my brother and me as young boys growing up, "where there is a problem, there is opportunity" and there will certainly be winners from Brexit, particularly in the fast moving SME world.

These winners will be the Brexitpreneurs.

Is it really that bad?

I voted to remain. Britain exiting the EU wasn't something that I've ever thought was a good idea, financially, politically or culturally.

Think about it. 28 nations coming together into one mutually beneficial 'club', working under a single market ideal, becoming the largest economy in the world, where policies and laws are enacted for the good of all countries and do not give a distinct advantage to any one country over another member – this has to be a great thing.

In my early entrepreneurial career, I saved fortunes in duties and in time due to un-restricted trade.

With that said, do we really feel it has worked?

Are we sure that German interests are not seen as more important than those of other smaller members' interests?

Are the farming laws really upheld by the French?

Are we delighted with how the markets and politicians have dealt with the Eurozone sovereign debt crisis, or the worst refugee problem since World War II?

Now that the decision to leave has happened, is it really that bad to have left the EU?

Let's explore some of the key issues.

No single market

As an EU member one of the biggest draws is the single market. The single market in its purest form works as one territory without any internal borders or other regulatory obstacles to the free movement of goods and services.

When we joined the single market, it was to help the UK grow within the EU and for the trading block as a whole to stimulate competition and trade, improve efficiency, and help cut prices.

To do this all member states have to act as one. The only trouble with this is that not all members are equal and not all economies are equal.

From the below graph taken from research conducted by the Bank of America and Merrill Lynch (BAML), it is clear that there is considerable division between the economic growth of the UK, Germany and the rest of the Eurozone.

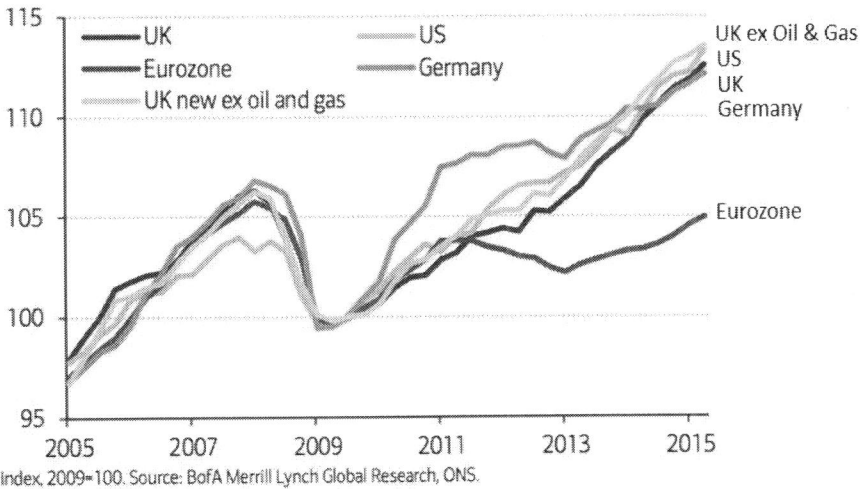

Index, 2009=100. Source: BofA Merrill Lynch Global Research, ONS.

Britain's economic GDP performance has more in common with the recovery in the US than the Eurozone. Removing the poor performing oil market (much of which is out of the UK's control), you will see an even more impressive recovery.

Compared to the Euro Zone it makes for very interesting reading.

Employment

In Britain, currently there is circa 5.5% unemployment. Inflation is low, the 'living wage' is being rolled out as the new benchmark as opposed to the lower 'minimum wage'.

Compare this to the unemployment rates in the rest of the Eurozone:

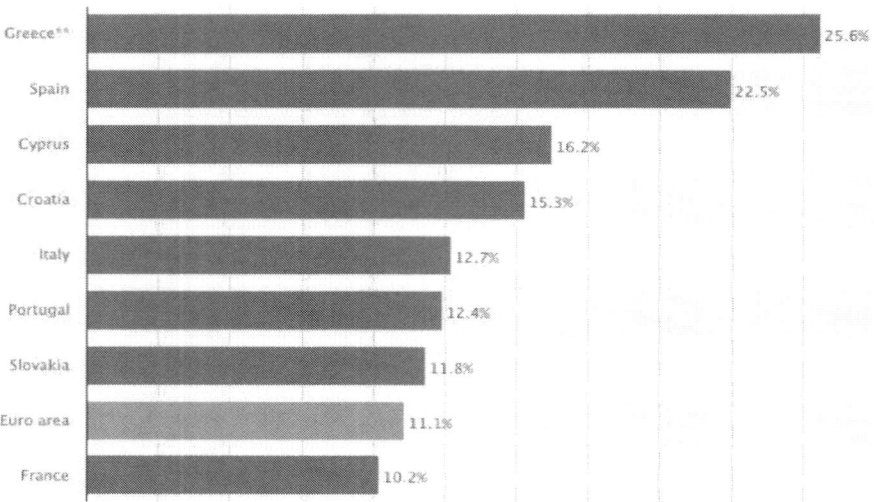

Source - Statista

If the single market did work, then unemployment should be the same figure across the whole of the EU.

An individual would simply move to where there is work or the work would go to where there were people out of work.

Yet it has not and it will not, because not all countries are equal.

Across the board some countries are propping up Europe's economic figures, while others are still stagnant or practically in recession.

Redistribution of wealth

The Eurozone debt crisis of 2009 has highlighted why there is a fiscal problem with the EU. Yes, the EU is part of a single market but it does not have a fiscal union to address underperforming areas.

In Britain, London has a GDP (gross domestic product) bigger than some smaller European countries, as a result it generates far greater amounts of wealth than other UK cities and regions. If another town like Liverpool is struggling, the money is redistributed by the UK government to pay for welfare or prop up the local economy.

Infrastructure, like new railway lines, can be installed to link cities and improve connections for people working or looking to expand their business. This is the case with projects like HS2 and HS3, designed to help build the 'Northern Powerhouse' to invest in and grow an economic hub to attract foreign businesses not just to London, but to Britain's other large cities. London-paid taxes are contributing to a central government who is re-distributing this wealth into Northern cities.

The EU is not able to act in the same way. They are able to lend money to Greece, but this is a loan and therefore requires repayments, and the repayments are hanging like a ball around the neck of all citizens of Greece.

A loan is not a re-distribution of wealth – it is a loan and therefore while putting a plaster onto a wound, the loan is only a quick fix for what are far deeper cracks for countries like Greece.

It is commonly thought that two, maybe three generations of Greeks will be paying back the mistakes of this generation. But how should a country like Greece solve the problem?

The simple solution is by creating more exports.

Countries who want to export more can usually do so quickly by devaluing their currency to make themselves good value to potential buyers. Which is exactly what being part of the single currency does not allow.

Greece are stuck needing to sell more internationally, but their currency is the same as everyone else's in Europe and they therefore can create no advantage.

On the flip side, the British pound took a historic hit when Britain voted to exit the EU, and the assessment of many currency traders and economic experts is that it will continue to trade low against the dollar and many other large non Euro currencies as it goes through Brexit and for the first few years following. This does have many negatives for Industry, but it does help significantly with exports, making the UK products and services extremely attractive.

It also makes UK assets very affordable with UK property and UK companies themselves seeing an influx in foreign investment.

This is one of the reasons why Britain has managed to keep the economy growing through this process.

Our tourists...

As tourists, our euro-hopping population have an unrelenting desire to go on culture cramming euro city breaks, beer guzzling excursions, skin scorching holidays all over the continent every year.

In fact, we Brits make over 50 million visits to Europe each year, some to do business, some for pleasure, others to fall out of bars, to the shame of us all.

All-in-all we accounted for more than a quarter of the tourism to Spain, just over 10% of tourism to Greece and a whopping 40% of tourism to Cyprus.

The British impact is wide-spread. Take Spanish hotelier giant Melia who rely immensely on the Brits abroad. Without our short break invasion each season to the Med, they would barely have a business to consider.

Then take all the Brits living in Spain and throughout the continent, many of them staying as British nationals spending their savings and pensions within the local European communities.

If they were to start feeling unwelcome and pushed back to Blighty, they will take their fortunes in spending power with them.

Whole communities built up around servicing the long term residential Brits, will crumble leaving Spanish ghost towns in their wake.

It just doesn't seem logical or a financially intelligent move for cash strapped Spain to start making life harder for our UK nationals to visit or remain long-term.

This position is echoed throughout Europe. They may not like it, but many of their coastal economies need the Brits.

You only have to look at the UK's own seaside towns to see what the reverse looks like. When cheap package holidays started and the ease of European travel began, the heyday of the British seaside died and coastal towns fell into disrepair and neglect. The Brits simply started spending their time and money on the

European mainland.

British seaside resorts are among the most deprived places in the country, blighted by high unemployment, poor health and riddled with crime. A 2017 report, from the Office for National Statistics, lays bare the 'crisis' facing resorts from Blackpool to Clacton, Ramsgate to Margate. It concludes that 'immediate regeneration is required' and that the heart of these towns needed to be 'saved'.

It comes after an earlier report, from the Centre for Social Justice, which said seaside towns have become 'dumping grounds' following the destruction of their economies by cheap foreign travel.

It was not by coincidence that the leave vote was so strong along the British coastline. It perhaps serves as a warning to European countries who do not value their British tourism levels.

For trade

In terms of trade, Britain imports almost a quarter of a trillion pounds' worth of goods from the EU27 nations, creating an £88.9 billion trade deficit with them (2015).

Germany, perhaps the most similar country to us on the continent, has a trade surplus with the other European members, earning far more from them than they do from Germany.

You can look at the overall figures and make the presumption that it will damage the countries who Britain buys from or visits for holiday the most, yet really when you break it down you have to look at the companies who are the backbone of these economies.

Far from trying to make political points and playing hard ball they have millions of global investors all of whom want this exit done, dusted and put behind them. They do not have the stomach for a long drawn out spaghetti western style exit, with years of economic and political hangovers.

They want it done and they want it done now.

The fact is that the transition period will help everyone, but even during this time strong agreements need to be made. If heels are dragged and restrictions on British trade and tourism put in place, there will be trade warnings issued to every exchange that Europe's biggest companies are listed on.

Think of the effect levies and duties would have on Telefonica's UK arm 02, Ferrovial's Heathrow, Santander's UK banking branches, Inditex's Zara. Think of Germany's E.ON, BMW, Volkswagen and Sweden's Skandia, Electrolux or Ericsson.

All of these companies UK operations contribute significant revenues to their European parents overall end-of-year financials.

Whichever way we look at it, the UK serves as an incredible asset to all its European trading block friends.

This creates a problem for Europe as they slap Britain on the wrist for being the disobedient child of the union.

As a result Britain is in an incredibly powerful position. Perhaps even the concept of having to pay to access the EU trading block is outlandish, and one our current and future negotiators should not be persuaded by.

What we do with this position of power is yet to be seen, but over the next 5 years it is our asset to use, and as Brexitpreneurs we should make sure the politicians do not fritter it away.

Brexit for the brave is the opportunity of a lifetime, and if we all only live once then this is the best opportunity we will get!

Brexit SWOT Analysis

On the 23rd June 2016, the news that Britain voted to Brexit had a whole number of different effects on the economy. The stock markets fell, the British banking sector was hit, and the British pound sank 20%, but I am sure that anyone who voted to leave would have been expecting that sort of short term dip.

As a Remainer, I definitely thought that there would be short and medium-term issues and was unsure on the long-term benefits, hence why I voted to remain.

Even though some part of EU legislation can sound a little ridiculous at times I still believe that there was an advantage in staying in the EU. We are after all a nation that depends on imports for energy and goods, and in turn being part of the EU we have a decent mechanism for trade.

However, is leaving really that bad either? – I think potentially as a nation it could create the opportunity we need, to go out there and become more relevant and autonomous, in the world, not just the EU.

Now it has happened, it is always important to plan for the future and to understand where the positives and also where the negatives lie for Britain as we move on from Brexit.

Many tools can be used to analyse situations and take decisions, but coming from a business background, I wanted to explore the application of one of these simple tools, the SWOT Analysis.

A SWOT analysis is a methods used to evaluate Strength (S), Weakness (W), Opportunities (O) and Threats (T) involved in innovative ideas and strategies.

It can be applied to products, services and strategies. These four factors evaluate both internal and external factors related to a specific project, idea or strategy.

It is usually drawn as follows, with each box having its elements added so that they can be weighed up against each other:

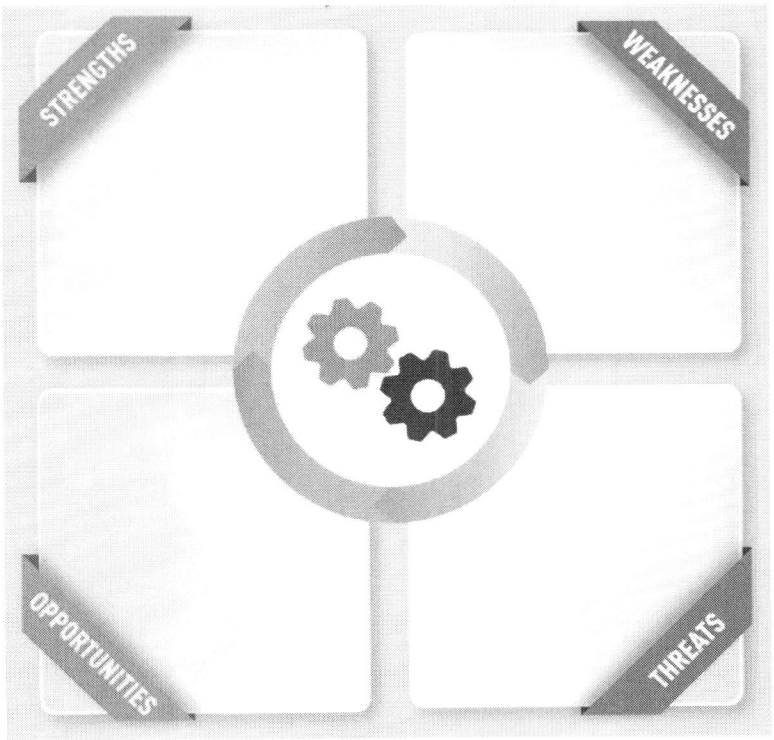

In this case, we are going to look at how it applies to Brexit to discover where we need to be careful but also where the opportunities are for Brexitpreneurs.

To start, let's define the four main factors in the tool:

Strengths (S) – The strength point in the argument for Brexit and the projected continued strengths of Britain's new global position.

Weaknesses (W) – The weakness in the argument for Brexit and their association with the threats that can be faced following Britain's exit.

Opportunities (O) – The opportunities that are now available and which may become available in the short, medium and long term.

Threats (T) – The threat that we will face following exit which may exist in the short, medium and long term.

Strengths

Below are the strengths of the Brexit decision:

1. Release restrictions on SMEs:

Small and medium enterprises (SMEs) did not receive many benefits from membership of the EU, yet they faced restrictions related to the trade regulations between EU member countries. By exiting the EU, SMEs will no longer be restricted by some of these regulations, which may have a positive impact on this important and largest part of the economy.

2. Sovereignty:

Being part of the EU, the UK does not have full control over its own borders and affairs. The UK gave up part of its control over decisions related to the borders in exchange for trade and other security benefits as one of the EU members.

While the UK is still bound by the membership of NATO, the UN, and the World Trade Organization, leaving the EU will give the UK more control over its own sovereignty.

3. Autonomy:

Leave campaigners stirred up British people's passion for independence. Robin Horsley, an active Leave Campaigner stated:

"Having the ability to be able to create circumstances for Britain's own benefit as opposed to being locked into a system that says, as a presupposition, that we're better off together, in fact just means compromise, compromise, compromise.

Autonomy is what it's about.

True Independence.

The ability to be able to make decisions, to be able to create circumstances for the prosperity of our own people."

4. More jobs, public service provision and housing:

Currently, there are 1.7m European and 2.93m international workers in the UK. This increasing number of immigrants has led to difficulties relating to housing, health care, transport, education and jobs.

Less people will mean the current system which is widely reported to be bursting at the seams, will be more fit for purpose.

5. Reduce terrorism:

With increasing security threats, it is commonly believed that staying in the EU would keep the door open for terrorism and security threats and would reduce the ability to control borders and monitor people.

However, it is important to stress that much of the new wave of terrorism is 'home grown' and therefore this only goes part way towards helping this problem (if at all).

6. Global Network of Embassies

The UK has one of the largest global networks of Embassies and diplomatic missions. In a letter to Lord Laming on the 20th October 2015, the then Minister of State at the Foreign and Commonwealth Office, Hugo Swire confirmed that the UK's aim is to be "the best-networked state in the world". This is a massive asset that will be in full use when we look to negotiate new trade deals globally.

7. Language

The UK has always aspired to remain a global player, there are many factors attached to that goal, but one of the best assets we have that keep us at the international table is language. English is considered the language of Business globally, which comes about as a consequence of history, a consequence of our imperial past.

The British empire does have negative associations for many international communities (quite rightly in most circumstances), but in today's world it has left us with this huge legacy of language that provides the foundations and opportunities for us to build upon.

8. Legal System

The UK is known as having one of the most effective legal systems in the world. In fact, global maritime law is based upon it, as are many national legal systems across the world.

When reflecting upon how other countries viewed the UK MP Michael Gove in my interview with him following the Brexit vote stated:

"From my conversations with political representatives globally, they thought fundamentally that in Britain you have the most effective legal sector in the world.

Britain is a place to which people come, to resolve their disputes, have their contracts sealed, to secure legal advice.

Our common law traditions, the quality of the law firms who are here, the incorruptible and reliable nature of our courts is a unique asset."

This becomes a key asset when attracting businesses and individuals to invest in projects, companies and property in the UK.

9. Britain's Soft Power

Britain's soft power is the cultural power that runs through international opinion of our nation. Everything from the BBC to the Royal Shakespeare Company, from the birth of pop, heavy metal, punk and grime to the invention of cricket, tennis and rugby (to name just a few).

People passionately support, follow and are fans of the current flag bearers of modern culture and when they look back in time the forefather is usually Britain, this is a feel good asset that cannot be ignored.

Weakness

Below are the suggested weaknesses of the Brexit decision

1. Reduce the flexible movement in EU countries

Under the EU umbrella, both academic and industry talent were able to move freely between EU countries, which has had a positive impact on the research and innovation in UK. This has allowed the UK to solidify its position as one of the leading countries in the field of innovation.

In a survey conducted by the Design Week Magazines, 98% of the designers who voted to remain in the EU are driven by the fear of recession, limited access to EU clients, and freedom of movement for talents.

2. Drop in Tax revenues

As 44% of UK trade is exported to EU countries (£240 billion out of £550 billion total exports in 2016). Brexit will have a significant impact on the tax revenues as the economy shrinks unless other markets are opened or the UK keeps its position as a member in the open trade agreement of the European Economic Area.

3. Loss of Jobs

In a comparison to jobs being seen as a strength of Brexit due to the uptake of UK jobs going to EU nationals, a South Bank University research paper estimated 3,445,000 UK jobs that "depend upon exports to the EU" may be lost as the UK leaves the EU - 2.5 million directly and 900,000 indirectly.

'Direct' employment is people employed in industries that export to the EU, 'indirect' relates to jobs that come about as a result of increased demand for products resulting from exporters' profits and their workers' wages.

These jobs are related to the trade between the UK and EU and while the whole number may not suffer unemployment with Brexit, many jobs will be affected due to the regulations related to visa and immigration laws between countries.

4. Finding talented workers

In an article by Professor Adrian Favell in the London School of Economics, he highlighted that the UK is one of the countries which benefits the most from the free movement of labour in the EU. Leaving the EU will shrink the number of candidates which companies can choose from.

5. Reduction in Exports

44% percent of the UK's exports go to EU countries, which has been spurred on by the tax free arrangements we have with the EU. This has decreased from closer to 50% in 2008, however it is a sizable chunk of what we sell as a nation.

Many experts believe that leaving the EU will contribute to shrinking the UK market and reduce its negotiating power as the

UK leaves its powerful seat at the EU members table.

6. UK's place in the World

Many remain campaigners continue to believe that being part of the EU contributed to the UK having more influence in Europe which can bring more benefits for the UK in comparison to its position outside of the EU.

7. Access to European countries

As part of the EU, Britons may live, work and stay in any of the EU countries. While English families may find university tuitions are expensive in UK, they can travel to other countries to get their degrees for lower cost (this does not apply in Scotland; the education and funding systems in Scotland are different from England). The British can also travel for tourism and trips around Europe with less cost and effort when compared to other countries outside the EU.

Opportunities

Below are the suggested opportunities of the Brexit decision

1. A global HQ

Leaving the EU creates an opportunity to renegotiate with every country in the world globally. Britain created free trade back in the commonwealth days and we have many relationships globally.

2. Membership fee

Leaving the EU would result in an immediate cost saving, as we would no longer contribute to the EU budget. Last year, Britain paid in £13bn, but it also received £4.5bn worth of spending, says Full Fact, "so the UK's net contribution was £8.5bn". That's just over 22% of what the Government spends on education each year which is a considerable amount.

3. UK place in the World:

In contrast to the Remain campaigners' belief, Britons who support Brexit believe that leaving the EU will help the UK to re-establish itself as one of the world leaders and an independent nation. Those supporting Britain's continued membership of the EU believe this point is a disadvantage which is highlighted in the Weakness section.

4. Trade missions

Our Embassies are an enviably well-established global network: using them as staging posts for trade missions is a fantastic opportunity for an internationally minded Brexitpreneur.

I was told an eye-opening story by a guy who runs one of the largest recruitment companies globally. He was setting up an office in South America and he'd contacted the embassy to ask if they would possibly help him meet some of the local influential business people, CEOs and representatives from the large companies in the capital city.

He duly arrived for this, for what he thought was probably going to be a series of meetings to find that the embassy had actually hosted an evening event and invited everybody conceivable to come along to this event. He had a chance that evening, to speak to all kind of key people in these large businesses. At the end of the evening, he said to the ambassador,

"Thank you so much. That was absolutely fantastic, way beyond my expectations."

The ambassador said, "This is what I'm here for, this is one of the key purposes of having an embassy but nobody knows about it so nobody ever contacts us, so when you did, we wanted to lay it out and make it a proper event."

I truly believe that examples like this are fewer than we think and the UK has such an untapped asset in its embassy's.

Threats

Below are the suggested threats of the Brexit decision:

1. Reduce the attraction of the UK market

One of the attractive factors in the UK economy is being part of the EU. Companies such as Nissan can build its factory in UK and export cars to all of the EU without paying any tariffs. After Brexit, the British economy may lose this advantage.

2. Skills shortage

It is common knowledge that much of the NHS and many other public sector services are propped up by non-UK national workers, be it from the EU or beyond, having an immigration freeze that does not handle the requirement for vital skills in many of the most important areas of public service is a vital piece of the puzzle.

3. New territory

No other country has ever left the EU and the fear of recession hit the stock markets. Confidence which is so vital for any trading be it in Canary Wharf or in physical export and import goods has to be high for the economy to boom. Even after a few hours following the referendum result the stock markets were dramatically affected and the pound sank to a 10% drop in its value, the lowest level since 1985.

SWOT Conclusion

With a final analysis of the strengths, weakness, opportunities and threats of the decision to leave the EU, we are where we are and there is nothing that a Brexitpreneur can do about the past.

Knowing the starting point is vital, that is where the growth begins, there of course there will be plenty of road blocks ahead but at least we know why.

My father talks about 'the fat bloke in the pub' it is a crude observation around what damage 'hearsay' and that 'know it all down the pub' can do for confidence and opinions.

The SWOT I hope gave you some balanced views upon the starting blocks. So now let's see where we can go from here.

CHAPTER 2

WE ARE GOING HERE

Getting back on the horse

Now that we understand what happened, it is time to think about getting up, dusting ourselves off and of course 'getting back on the horse'.

The Brits have always been excellent at the 'stiff upper lip', even in our darkest days with the Blitz raining terror across the country, the everyday man and woman displayed courage in the face of adversity.

The globe has always perceived us as having courage under fire, or doing our bit for the greater good. That 'do your duty and show no emotion' attitude was expressed in Lord Tennyson's, The Charge of the Light Brigade:

> Theirs not to make reply,
>
> Theirs not to reason why,
>
> Theirs but to do and die:
>
> Into the valley of Death
>
> Rode the six hundred.

I still get shivers up my spin when I read those 5 lines, to think of six hundred men riding to certain death 'for king and country'.

It is these types of story and sense of duty that we have grown up with that have shaped much of how we are culturally.

American friends who I have spoken to were so shocked that we would vote for something that was counter to our economic benefits, they told me that it simply would not have happen in the USA as everyone votes with their wallets in mind.

I of course retort, "let's see how Trump plays out in the end", but that's for another time and different book!

There are many cultures who are considered to be outwardly emotional, the Brits are considered to be the opposite. This I believe will be one of our greatest strengths as we regain the trust of economies all over the world. If we are calm, confident and positive then it will put others at ease around us.

It's time to 'Keep Calm and Carry On'.

What does Brexit mean for entrepreneurs?

The term Brexitpreneurship I coined at the start of this book to help frame the need for business owners to change their actions and thinking around growth in the next few years.

I think it is fundamental when you're looking at points of change to really start thinking about it in the right way. A way that is relevant to you and one in which you might be able to use information to shape your future.

I've always been an entrepreneur, I've always thought that politics is better left for the politicians. I don't have the stomach for the political arguments. I love understanding it, I love the drama, I love the politics. But I can't get involved personally. For me, I'm an empire creator, a money generator, an entrepreneur. I love challenge and adversity. Knowing what the world will look like when we get to Brexit will be extremely helpful when spotting opportunities.

2020 Trends

As Brexit will take us to the dawn of the next decade, let's look at what the world will look like in 2020.

This will be an exciting new era for technology and the internet as we see it maturing. From the birth of the internet, when Brit, Tim

Berners-Lee officially invented the World Wide Web in March 1989, to its infant years of the 90's, then to what we have just experienced in the last two decades, the teenage decades. By the time we hit 2020 the internet will reach young adulthood, where we will be hyper connected and the generation using and developing the 'things' that use it would have never known a world that did not have the internet.

Gen Y

One of the biggest challenges for businesses heading out of Brexit and into 2020 is integrating the Millennials or Gen Y into a Baby Boomer culture.

Gen Y were born between 1977 and 1998 and are 75 million strong in size. They see a world without borders, they are totally mobile and take to technology like a duck to water. They are global citizens and according to YouGov as many as 73% voted to remain in the EU.

By 2020 it is estimated that they will make up half the workforce and will be the driving force in the labour market as well as moving into entrepreneurial roles and leadership positions. They will be the 'doers' as we push through Brexit.

They commonly blame the baby boom generation for making Brexit happen against their will and many of the people who publicly came out to say that they regret their leave vote (which they saw as a protest vote) were Gen Y.

However, for many of Gen Y they were raised by baby boomers who doted on them, giving them an ample supply of attention and validation.

This has led to high expectations and self-confidence which makes them believe they are highly valuable to any organisation from day one. They usually find out they are not with a bump and tend to move on from their first and second 'proper job' relatively quickly.

They also have found that their university education does not mean what it used to mean in the job market, leaving them with large debts and misguided expectations.

However, they will be the best equipped generation we have ever had to handle a global-looking economy after Brexit.

They are the 'can do' generation, the 'tech start up' culture, never worrying about failure, never worrying about getting into debt to make things happen, never worrying about losing everything, because for many of them, they have already been through it all as broke university students during the last recession.

Their parents installed a sense of 'education is a good thing' combined with limitless knowledge and information sources upon the internet, they are great problem solvers, they are extremely focused on developing themselves and thrive on learning new job skills.

When it comes to work life balance, Gen Y have been described as 'lightweight nomads' not willing to give up their lifestyle for a career. They have travelled extensively and value having flexibility in their daily lives, they understand expensive possessions, cars and mortgages weigh them down and see technology such as Airbnb, zip car and Uber as ways of getting around the need to live in two up two down lifestyles like their baby booming parents.

It is trends and advances in technology that has led a whole generation into becoming global and in turn well placed to handle Brexit.

Gen Y are also team-oriented, in school they were taught lessons using a cooperative learning style, they feel comfortable working with others and want to make friends with the people at work. They believe that a team can accomplish more and create a better end result.

They also grew up in a multi-cultural Britain which has meant they are better than any generation working as part of global projects with cultures different to theirs.

They communicate in snippets through instant messaging, texting, Facebook, WhatsApp and e-mail, which enables quick and efficient communication not necessarily face-to-face again suiting international businesses.

Social media is at the heart of their ecosystem allowing them to connect with co-workers and friends around the world at great speed.

With 75 million Gen Y's entering the workplace Britain is lucky to have these free thinking, innovative, tech savvy individuals making up the building blocks of the work force.

They will bear the brunt of the all the bad that Brexit has to offer, let's just hope that they have the stomach for the fight because they definitely have the talents.

We Know Who but What about How

If Gen Y is our pool of up and coming talent, then what tools will they have to shape our brave new world?

Virtual Reality

To say that the consumer electronics industry has changed everything would be an understatement on par with calling World War II a minor skirmish.

We live in a world where people are willing to queue for days, just to be the first to get their hands on the latest version of their favourite device.

Those devices don't just do one thing either. They allow us to connect with people around the globe in ways that would have been impossible just a few years ago, using images, video and text in innovative ways.

More than that though, technology has become the catalyst for the next phase of innovation both in our personal lives and in business.

Think virtual reality headsets are for gamers? Think again, by 2020 Facebook's Oculus Rift and HTC Vive, will break out of gaming and be used to create a multitude of applications that will be so ground breaking that the traditional industries that we all know and love will be well and truly shaken up.

Think about all that time you have wasted in the past viewing properties to buy or rent, that were obviously not right when you viewed them, but looked great on the website. Or hotel rooms which you would have never booked if you had known, it was that small, or had that view.

Have you ever fancied driving a supercar? ...or maybe just test driving the latest BMW ahead of making a decision if it is time to change cars.

All of the above activities usually require multiple slots of time to go to places, see something, experience something, then in some cases realise that it is not right, and move on.

Saving time has always been an amazing driver for technology, and that is why by 2020 this will be reality, a virtual reality.

The last time we saw a shift like this was in the late 1800's with the invention of the fundamental technologies behind recording and broadcasting moving pictures and sound. Out of those technologies evolved radio, cinema, television, the telephone, the internet; all spawning a multitude of new industries, media formats and storytelling languages in the process.

The modern world, the world you and I know, wouldn't exist without the arrival of those technologies more than 150 years ago.

We are at one of these extraordinary moments again.

The world of entertainment exists to tell stories. We sit in the dark in a cinema and immerse ourselves into that story; we are taken along emotional roller coasters and by the end of the 2-hour film we feel totally satisfied and delighted.

By 2020 we will become part of that story; we will be standing with the characters, more like playing a part in someone else's dream. Plots and storylines will unfold, but you and your friends will be an active part in it.

As a Brexitpreneur do not laugh off virtual reality as a fad, many did the same when they thought about a TV, the internet or social media "it will never catch on…" was the concessions of many at the time.

By 2020 Virtual Reality will be a norm.

Today it is a fad for gamers and the early adopting business owners. Already the UK is a leading producer with many tech start up's and even tradeshows dedicated to the technology, my advice to you is go along, see what they have to say and try to spot how your industry will shift.

…I did, and I found a company called VR Drop and Share who created 360 degree photos that wrap around you and then through a screen share software and voice over IP (internet telephone calls) you are able to move a user from photo to photo explaining what is going on in each area – a little bit like a Virtual Reality Webinar, very interesting for my Property Clients and all done through a free app on a phone and cardboard goggles (a take on Google Cardboard), so therefore cost effective.

3D Printing

One place where technologies role as a catalyst for innovation is particularly evident is 3D printing.

This is the creation of a 3D printed object using additive processes.

In an additive process an object is created by laying down successive layers of material until the object is created. Each of these layers can be seen as a thinly sliced horizontal cross-section of the eventual object. Essentially a printer prints the same picture over and over adding a new layer each time and slowly building it into a 3D shape, the results are ground breaking.

According to global tech research company Gartner, we are in the beginnings of a "Digital Industrial Revolution" that threatens to reshape how physical goods are created and 3D printing is at the heart of it.

Authorities in the field believe that by 2020, 3D printing will result in the loss of at least £100-billion per year in intellectual property globally.

By 2020 major manufacturers both in the East and West will claim to have had intellectual property stolen for a mainstream product such as a Dyson vacuum cleaner or a NutriBullet blender or even the 3D printers themselves by thieves using advanced product scanners and 3D printers.

Most notable it will be 'hackers' from the same western markets rather than from China, who will simply be uploading the printable scans to the internet, much like the hackers did in the wiki leaks scandal.

The plummeting costs of 3D printers, scanners and 3D modelling technology, combined with improving capabilities, makes the feasibility for IP theft more accessible to would-be criminals.

On a more progressive note, by 2020, 3D printing of tissues and organs (bio-printing) will cause a global debate about regulating the technology or banning it for both human and non-human use.

Bioprinting is the medical application of 3D printers to produce living tissue and organs. The day when 3D bio printed human organs are readily available is drawing closer.

The emergence of 3D bio printing facilities with the ability to print human organs can leave people wondering what the effect of it will be on society. Beyond these questions, however, there is the reality of what 3D bio printing means in helping people who need organs that are otherwise not readily available. Does this spell the end of lung cancer as a new lung can be printed? Kidney transplants? Blindness?

It is all feasible when you think that these are simple biological parts that can be replicated as long as the brain and the body does not reject the new versions.

As someone who has a retinal vein occlusion in my left eye and has to have an injection into my pupil every 6 weeks to prevent me from going blind, I am all for the advancements in bio printing especially with the latest advancement in the bio printing of a full optic nerve.

I may not be first on the waiting list for a new eye, but I will not be far behind!

The Internet of Things

By 2020, there will be tens of billions of data-producing devices connected to the Internet, they are already changing how we live and work, but by the end of the decade the world will be so interconnected, we will wonder why we spend so much time, driving, parking and walking the aisles of Tesco.

This advancement will be driven by better sensor technology, linked up to many different types of machines that gather, store and analyse data and since they're all linked to the Internet, they can upload that data for further processing, download updated software and often be controlled from afar.

We are already using them in 1,000's of day to day smart tools such as smart cars, smoke detectors, door locks, industrial robots, streetlights, heart monitors, trains, wind turbines, even tennis racquets and kettles.

By 2020, Gartner estimates there will be 25 billion of these smart devices, transmitting tiny amounts of data to us, to the cloud and to each other.

Europe's largest engineering company, Siemens, has said the Internet of things is starting to power a fourth Industrial Revolution (after steam, electricity and wired computers).

Let's look at some of the internet of things' categories that the Brexitpreneur will be able to make use of as the UK powers out of Brexit and into 2020:

Smart-Home

For a few years we have been promised fridges that reorder your weekly shop for you, but it was not the technology that stood in its way, it is the supermarkets who are un-incentivised to lend their distribution and massive supply chain to this earth shattering development.

After all what would Tesco's do with all those mega stores? But after seeing what Uber has done to the taxi market and the rise of meal plan boxes delivered to your door such as Hellofresh and Gusto, by 2020 this will be a certain seismic shift and all it takes to kick off the war on the smart fridge is for an Apple or a Google type business to jump on it, or for a supermarket to lead the charge.

By 2020 the out of town mega supermarkets will be struggling and you will start to see their redevelopment into housing estates as the over exposed chains have to retrench and realign themselves to the dawn of the smart home.

There will of course still be a demand for in town convenience stores and smaller shops as people buy their lunch and bits and bobs when out and about, but the world would have changed.

Perhaps the most likely breakthrough will be Amazon, who have launched a line of branded buttons you can stick around your house to enable you to order home-staples like laundry detergent and toilet paper with one push. It also has its play in the home automation terminal space through Alexa who you can ask to order products purely through your voice.

One breakout smart home success to date, particularly among the many serious products aiming to reduce consumer electricity bills, is the Nest Learning Thermostat.

With a clean design, a simpler interface than existing programmable thermostats and backing from Google (which paid $3.2 billion for the start-up in 2013), Nest has been making dramatic inroads in Canada, the UK and the US.

Nest boasts that its device, which 'learns' your schedule, programs itself and can be controlled from your phone, could save users 20% on energy.

There are some legacy companies providing whole-home solutions. New Jersey based Crestron, sets up bespoke systems so clients can manage their security, energy use, lighting, HVAC and entertainment systems from their tablets.

The other way this shift will happen by 2020 is through mass collaboration, and leading the charge is Apple, who have release HomeKit, a platform it hopes developers in the smart-home sphere will use to create device-controlling apps. The aim is to provide one gateway, one platform, for the industry.

Smart-Office

Changes are coming to the office building, as well, which will have an unexpected level of bottom-line efficiency and worker convenience.

One mind-blowing example is from Cisco, who foresees a day when an executive driving into the office carpark, will automatically signal the elevator to come pick her up and turn on the lights in her office, have the coffee machine make her favoured first drink of the morning, turn on her computer and load the first few publications, blogs, software's she likes to look at when she first sits down.

In fact Cisco are creating this system to be so smart that it will prioritise elevators, coffee makers, printers and other communal machines to people based upon their cost per minute to the company. Therefore the more senior you are, the shorter your wait time for your morning latte. This not only creates an efficient place to work, but also saves minutes a day and ultimately days every year, allowing for better productivity and clear return on investment for Cisco.

Smart-Cities

More than half of the world's people now live in urban centres, and almost two-thirds of us will do so by 2050, which means 2.5 billion more city-dwellers to house, employ and transport.

That's a nightmare scenario for today's cities, plagued, as so many are, by traffic, pollution, crime, overflowing bins; but technologies being tested right now will help the cities of the future better cope with the looming migration.

Traffic lights with embedded video sensors can adjust their greens and reds according to where the cars are and the time of day. They're a double-win, reducing both congestion and pollution, since vehicles waiting at red lights burn up to 17% of the fuel consumed in urban areas.

In Barcelona's Born Market, sensors embedded into parking spaces relay real-time information on empty spots to an app for would-be parkers. Siemens recently gave a grant to a start-up devoted to building parking drones that could guide cars to available spots. Sounds insignificant? It's not: Up to 30% of congestion is caused by drivers cruising the streets in search of a place to park.

By 2020 we will have solar-powered bins on the side of the road, that crush waste and send a signal to a dispatcher requesting pickup when they're full, which aim to reduce the number of weekly rubbish collecting shifts, savings on fuel, maintenance and labour costs.

Smart-Vehicles

Elon Musk's latest-generation Tesla electric cars can travel up to

643 kilometres on a single charge. If you're getting low on electrical charge, the car's navigation system can lead you to the nearest charging station.

Tesla's comes equipped with Autopilot, which uses a combination of camera, radar and 360-degree sonar sensors to automatically drive on open roads and in stop-and-go traffic.

It also can not only find, but back into, parallel parking spots. The camera also reads posted speed limits and can warn drivers to slow down.

If you veer out of your lane and the driver's seat shakes the car's software enables it to warn the driver when other vehicles are sitting in their blind spots and to automatically dim the high beams when another car approaches.

Elon Musk's legacy will not be Tesla in this space, it will be the fact that he forced all the other car manufacturing giants to stand up, take notice and change, based upon Tesla's success. This, not Tesla itself, is how Musk will help save the world from global warming.

Players like Mercedes-Benz are now forced to launch smart-vehicles. In fact, they are currently perfecting a model that can interact with a smartphone, gathering information on your appointments, then proposing the quickest routes using real-time traffic information.

By 2020 it is estimated that there will be 250 million connected cars on the world's roads, with many of them capable of driving themselves.

There are eight million traffic accidents each year and 1.3 million crash-related deaths; Cisco's Smart, Connected Vehicles division suggests that autonomous cars could eliminate as many as 85% of head-on collisions.

They could also help ease traffic, since they'll be able to communicate their positions to each other and therefore drive much closer together than vehicles piloted by humans. Traffic experts call this "platooning" ie. packing more cars into the same road space and it could help save drivers at least some of the 90 billion hours they currently spend stuck in jams each year, generating 220 million metric tonnes of carbon-equivalent and wasting at least $1 trillion in fuel costs and lost productivity.

Mind blowing!

Smart-Healthcare

The baby boom generation is aging and the percentage of the population aged over 65 years is getting larger and larger every single year.

By 2020 this market will be massive and technology designed to help baby boomers live at home longer will be a trillion pound industry.

Already a new generation of sensors have been developed that can identify deterioration in condition of patients living at home and communicate that to their health care teams.

Philips, best known for light bulbs and electric toothbrushes, has created a pillbox that pops open when it's time to take your meds and sends a message to a family member or nurse confirming that the patient has taken them.

Smart-Beds are already being used in hospitals to let nurses know immediately if a patient has risen or left the bed entirely.

This technology will continue to advance and by 2020 the sensors will use high-definition cameras to monitor skin colour, breathing and temperature and alert nurses of any changes. These devices will eventually help doctors and nurses care for and monitor more patients both at home and in hospital beds.

Then there's the booming market for fitness trackers like the FitBit, Apple Watch, Suunto and others, which has already surpassed $2 billion, with well over 84 million sold so far.

These monitors measure heart rate, sleep patterns, diet, exercise and more. The devices then beam that data to mobile apps. Soon, that information could be sent directly to your health care provider or insurer, which currently still rely on your promise that you exercise four times a week!

By 2020 many UK health care providers will offer clients % off premiums if they willingly hand over data that proves they lead a healthy lifestyle. Vitality Health are already leading the way by offering Vitality points for their members to spend on face creams, gym membership and spa breaks if they submit their fitness data.

Smart-Energy

The basic theory behind Smart-Energy or the Smart-Grid is simple: Power is priced on the basis of demand and this information is transmitted immediately to offices and homes with smart-meters, thermostats and appliances so that they can draw the power they need at off-peak times, when it's cheapest.

This system uses market forces to balance the system loads and will make power networks less susceptible to blackouts.

By 2020 your Smart-Thermostat will receive daily information on energy pricing and select the most cost effective tariffs accordingly.

The growth of renewable energy sources also hinges in a large part on the smart grid. By 2020, according to the International Energy Association, renewables will replace natural gas as the world's second-largest source of power (coal is still on top).

Here in Britain, wind and solar are by far the fastest-growing power-generating sectors (though they still account for just a few per cent of the total). While they may be easier on the environment, they put major pressure on the grid, since the energy generated by solar and wind farms varies by time of year and day, throwing out of whack its delicate balancing act. Solar panels that can communicate the amount of power they are generating already exist, but by 2020 we would have developed a scalable battery solution to store overflow when we don't need it. Add to that Tesla's latest pivot into roof tiles, the next wave will bring solar into its second great growth phrase, seeing the rooftops of 1,000's of buildings upgraded into mini solar farms all adding into the smart-grid.

The latest generation of wind turbines are also benefiting from Internet of Things technology. GE-built turbines on the leading edge of a wind farm can let those behind them know that a gust is coming, prompting them to immediately alter the angle of their blades to protect themselves from damage and lengthen their lives. A relatively new software program also processes the data collected by turbine sensors and proposes the optimal angles to generate more power, increasing wind-farm production by as much as 5%.

Smart-Agriculture

Agriculture is becoming interconnected and smarter with the rise of the internet of things new machines from John Deere not only plough, sow and reap, they can also collect data, including air and soil temperatures, moisture, wind speed, humidity, solar radiation and rainfall.

Smart watering systems already sprinkle just enough water on the fields, in just the right places, and can detect leaks in water pipes, vital in hot dry summers and simple for cost savings and efficiencies.

One company has developed a sensor that can detect high counts of a particular pest and then release pheromones to disrupt their mating rituals, which can in turn, reduce the need for pesticides.

Even cows are now transmitting bits of data in real time: A Dutch company has created sensors that, when attached to individual animals, can tell farmers which ones are on heat, pregnant or ill.

This continuous flow of data, combined with the fashion of 'farm to table living' where consumers want to know the entire supply chain story (and the best stories are always when the food comes from only 30 miles away) is going to help bring the British Agricultural industry back into profit.

Smart-Wearables

Wearable computing, or wearables, is quickly moving into mainstream society, led by the growing, multi-billion-pound health and fitness markets (think about the Nike+, Fitbit and the Jawbone Up). By 2020, consumer wearables will become more sophisticated, capturing what the user sees, hears or even feels through biorhythmic responses. The technical hurdles that have stalled the adoption of wearables (battery life, augmented reality, chip evolution and bandwidth) are quickly eroding; opening doors to creative minds determined to exploit this technology for commercial gain as evidenced by sizable investments in wearable technology from Samsung, Google, Apple and Microsoft.

Cryptocurrency

Cryptocurrencies such as Bitcoin, Litecoin and Etherium is a digital currency for which encryption techniques are used to regulate its use and generate its release. Unlike normal currencies such as pounds, dollars, euros and yen, cryptocurrency is not regulated or controlled by any bank, government or centralised financial authorities.

Instead, it relies on the power of the Internet to guarantee its value and confirm transactions. Users on a network verify every transaction, and those transactions then become a matter of public record. This prevents the same digital currency or coin from being spent twice by the same person.

Because of their lack of supply and the prevention of a central organisation such as a government to 'print' more, cryptocurrencies are best described as digital gold. They are essentially sound value that is secure from political influence.

Cryptocurrencies are also a fast and comfortable means of payment with a worldwide scope, and they are private and anonymous enough to serve as a means of payment for black markets and any other outlawed economic activity.

But while cryptocurrencies are used for payment of goods and services, its use as a means of speculation and a store of value dwarfs the payment aspects currently.

Cryptocurrencies gave birth to an incredibly dynamic, fast-growing market for investors and speculators. Exchanges like Coinbase, Kraken or Shapeshift enables the trade of hundreds of cryptocurrencies. Their daily trade volume exceeds that of major European stock exchanges.

In this rich ecosystem of coins and token, you experience extreme volatility. Its common that a coin gains 10 percent in a day, sometimes 100 percent, just to lose the same the next day. If you are lucky, your coin's value grows up to 1,000 percent in one or two weeks.

What is the future of Cryptocurrency?

In the next few years leading up to 2020 the market of cryptocurrencies will be fast and wild. Nearly every week we will see new cryptocurrencies emerge, others will die, early adopters get wealthy and late investors lose money.

Every new cryptocurrency will come with a promise, mostly a big story to turn the world around.

Few new coins will survive the first months and most will be pumped and dumped by speculators and live on as zombie coins until the last bagholder loses hope ever to see a return on his investment.

Yet this massive surge of investment and global adoption will see a new super wealthy emerge. Early adopting 'geeks' who decided to get involved in the 'revolution' right at the start only to be absolutely proved right and find themselves multi-millionaires in a matter of years.

By 2020 cryptocurrencies will have gained legitimacy as a protocol for business transactions and micropayments. They will overtake companies like Western Union as the preferred remittance tool.

The wild west of Cryptocurrencies will become completely main stream. The current price bubble will burst and inflated currencies such as Bitcoin will crash, but out of the back of the crash will be the greatest recovery an innovation has ever seen since the dotcom bubble of the 90's.

The value of each coin will also grow far higher than their pre-crash position.

People all over the world buy Bitcoin to protect themselves against the devaluation of their national currency. By 2020 countries such as Argentina or Angola will hit 1,000% per week inflation and currency meltdown.

Shopkeepers, in order to buy and sell bread and pay their employees, will have to switch to Bitcoins with QR codes on their smartphones, because Argentinian Pesos or Angolan Kwanza will be worthless.

Once you can pop out to the shops to buy your weekly shopping with a stable and global currency, very quickly you will see an entire nation switch over to Bitcoin.

And it will never go back.

Minor currencies all over the world will be under threat of extinction. It may sound dramatic, but it is no different to the fate of the Zimbabwean Dollar, which was the official currency of Zimbabwe from 1980 to 12 April 2009.

During this time, it was subject to periods of above-average inflation, followed by a period of hyperinflation which reduced it to one of the lowest valued currency units in the world.

It was redenominated three times (in 2006, 2008 and 2009), with up to $100 trillion new banknotes issued, but it was too late and the currency was effectively abandoned on 12 April 2009.

In its place, the United States dollar became the most commonly used currency because it was available and stable.

If this happened today, you can bet against a switch to the US dollar, after all you will have to carry notes and coins around and have a bank account, something very difficult to achieve for a vast percentage of the world's population.

In his book 'The Millennium Development Goals and Human Rights: Past, Present and Future' Malcolm Langford observes:

"Currently 70 per cent of the world's population lives in countries

with incomplete registration of births"

He goes on to comment

"Birth registration importance is borne out in practice. It is often a precondition for accessing formal legal identity documents, such as passports, national ID cards and accessing credit and financial institutions and their services such as bank accounts"

Without bank accounts, it is very hard for a member of the population to start to pull themselves out of poverty, yet with cryptocurrencies the requirement for bank accounts is not there.

Better still for war torn countries or in dictator lead regions, the population can have their bank accounts frozen or money changing hands can be tracked, all of which are unpopular to all cross sections of a population.

And once a country like Argentina makes the switch, then all the other countries who are in the same predicament will switch too and just like the dominoes of the Internet and the smart phone fell, so will the dominoes of cryptocurrencies.

This will make for a massive market cap upon bitcoin and an even larger price valuation.

As a Brexitpreneur knowing that a huge percentage of the globe will be going crypto can be an extremely useful thing.

If you can gear yourself up to accept it as payment or even

innovate into the space with service and product offerings, then you will be able to get the jump on the mass population.

Britain prides itself on its financial services but if we want to stay relevant and at the forefront of this new world, we must adapt very quickly to this global opportunity because by 2020 it will already be too late.

CHAPTER 3

THIS IS HOW YOU WIN

There has never been a better time for Brexit

As an entrepreneur, there has never been a better time for Brexit.

Many of us may have voted against it.

Many of us will have to deal with all the red tape and economic uncertainty that it brings.

But let's face it, if this happened in 2007 we would be on our knees by now. A global recession followed by a Brexit would have been an economic disaster.

Even if it was the booming 1980's where the country was buoyant, without the internet, international trade would have not been as simple as it is for our hyper connected world of today.

This book is about knowing where we are, knowing where we are going, then winning.

I refuse to cry over spilt milk in this final chapter, as entrepreneurs we do not do that. We are used to the fast pace of change.

Now that we can draw a line under the decision to leave and we are not deluded to think that the UK economy will be shaken up, I want to introduce to you what I see at the most important areas for you to focus upon in the oncoming months.

Some of the 11 steps may seem obvious, but from meeting with 1,000's of business owners in the last 10 years, I know that many of the recommendations are not being implemented.

Other recommendations will require you to consider fundamental shifts in how you approach your Brexit business. So even if you think it does not apply to you, do think deeply - after all Blockbuster once thought that renting movies online would never catch on; until it did catch on, by then it was too late for them.

Do not let preconceptions sleepwalk you into similar mistakes.

The 11 steps to winning at Brexit

1. Positivity attracts like a magnet
2. Get a mentor and be a mentor
3. What gets measured gets improved
4. Brand Britain
5. Think Globally
6. Innovate, Innovate, Innovate
7. Demonstrate thought leadership
8. Negotiate and Do Deals
9. Use Government incentives
10. Celebrate the Success of your Customers
11. Be relentless

1. Positivity attracts like a magnet

A positive attitude is attractive and like a magnet can make opportunity gravitate towards you, particularly if many others around you are being down beat and negative, which seems to be the go to position of the business and media community when discussing Brexit.

As Brits, we can easily slip into a 'moan', just think about the last time you discussed the weather with anyone, the predisposition is to negative frame it as 'too hot', 'too cold' and almost certainly 'too wet'.

Misery loves company, and miserable people quickly realise that they don't win many allies. Positive-minded people, on the other hand, tend to attract the voluntary support of others. That collaborative network helps drive their success, which in turn makes other people keep wanting to work with and associate with them, including in trying times.

The trouble is, many of us don't really know what to do with 'stay positive' advice, believing instead that our temperament isn't something we can really control. But with practice, we can learn to adjust our attitudes to make them work in our favour more often.

None of us can be relentlessly upbeat all the time, but a positive mind-set can be indispensable when the going gets tough.

The key, of course, isn't to become eternally optimistic. No one can uphold a sunny disposition 100% of the time. But you don't have to. Instead, learning to think positively in the face of adversity when times really get tough is both the more useful and more achievable approach when it comes to winning from Brexit.

From looking at the changes in my life, I can say without a doubt that remaining positive has been my greatest asset.

Here are a few ways being optimistic has helped me grow my business and can assist you.

Your Team

I truly believe that as an entrepreneur you are the sum total of an excellent team, be it an in-house team or an outsourced team, no successful entrepreneur is an island!

An improvement I started making with my team is catching myself when I start complaining or have negative thoughts. Data suggests that when employees are happy, they produce better work. As leaders, it's essential that we keep this in mind.

I always feel that if someone makes a mistake or falls behind, its best to not bring down the individual, but to review the process and system as a whole and make changes to it with the individual, so that they give you their buy in and you can also see if you as the leader can shoulder some of the blame for the issue.

It's astonishing to see how much a company culture is built off the attitude of the leader. When the captain is in a bad mood, the entire crew suffers. While this cripples companies that have angry bosses, it is a weapon for those who can remain optimistic. Be the example of the positivity you want to see in your team, and watch productivity increase dramatically.

Believe in your talents even when you fail

There has never been a successful entrepreneur who has not experienced failure. Positive leaders know that they need to take risks and push their boundaries, which can at times result in failure.

When I set up my business I was buying 40ft shipping containers worth of products I had designed, manufactured in India and China and had shipped to the UK.

Many months I would have 1,000's of products at sea which by hook or by crook I had to sell before the container landed in the UK otherwise it would mean massive cash flow and warehousing issues.

I was always proud that I was able to achieve this, except for when I didn't.

The 2007 recession hit and I had a warehouse full of wacky photo frames, tartan piggy banks and spotty rubber bath ducks. None of my clients were buying anything, particularly my untested new ranges. We were sitting on big debts and loads of stock.

Undeterred I set out to do anything I could to get further orders from my clients, including re-dressing their window displays, creating free promotion flyer designs for their shops and even helping them build a new website in exchange for their orders of photo frames and ducks.

Many of my competitors went bust during this time, but we tried everything to help market our clients in exchange for their continued support. We did so well, they started recommending us to their friends so we could help market their businesses, or build them a website. This became an opportunity we hadn't foreseen.

Due to our positivity and energy, we found ourselves being able to charge for our 'help' which quickly became our 'marketing' services.

Subsequently our marketing business was born and from this potentially business ending place our positively helped us to now build our award winning marketing agency.

Brexitpreneurs need to positively approach new challenges with the belief that either they'll succeed or take something useful from a potential stumble that will help them do better next time.

The start-up world may have nurtured a certain obsession with productive failure that may be overblown. But while failure can't teach us absolutely everything we need to succeed, it can help define for us what we are good at and what still needs work.

Be Grateful

Help share your positivity by thanking those who have helped you along the way and always make sure you give credit where it's due.

Brexit will offer some tough times and many new opportunities, as entrepreneurs we tend to spend our time thinking about the future, always looking for new challenges, yet do not disregard the need to always be grateful for what you already have.

Brexitpreneurs need to stay aware of and be grateful for the gifts that have been bestowed upon them. After all, some of the most important things in life aren't those we earn, they're given to us by those who care about us. It's only a mind-set steeped in gratitude that goes any way toward making us worthy of them.

Humour

One way to cultivate this sort of positivity is to use humour (tactfully) to brighten up situations and see silver linings in circumstances that look discouraging. This type of mind-set prevents you from blaming others and pushes you toward solutions instead.

We have always used humour in my businesses, in fact my business partner and brother Tim is renowned for his terrible jokes in the office. They do seem lighten everyone's mood in times of high pressure or deadlines, they have a reverse effect on me but that is the beauty of working with your brother I guess!

2. Get a Mentor and be a Mentor

Highly successful people are never satisfied with what they already know. They're often attending lectures, reading or listening to audiobooks and podcasts, finding new ways to hone their existing skills and pick up new ones.

Not only do they have mentors who push them to do better and challenge their ideas, they also tend to mentor others.

Being driven by your passions and surrounding yourself with people on all sides who do the same is a powerful defence against adversity and gives you momentum as you negotiate what Brexit throws at you.

No one is too good or too successful to have a mentor.

You are never too old, clever or experienced to have a mentor.

The biggest names in business have always had mentors and taken advice and guidance from their mentors. For instance, Bill Gates, Oprah Winfrey and Mark Zuckerberg all have had mentors and still have them.

The more you understand the process of mentoring, the more you realise that it's no surprise that some of the most successful and influential people in the world can easily tie their defining moments in life back to a strong mentoring relationship they had or still have.

A mentor will also help you to open doors; empower you, engage and enable you to focus on your goals, help you to realise what you are capable of achieving regardless of the challenges you foresee.

"Mentoring is to support and encourage people to manage their own learning in order that they may maximise their potential, develop their skills, improve their performance and become the person they want to be." – Eric Parsloe, the Oxford School of Coaching and Mentoring

For me having someone I trust that I can bounce ideas off is invaluable and at any time I have a number of mentors that I go to for different questions, usually based upon their skill-set / experience and the type of issue I am struggling with.

I have also found mentoring others has in its own way made me a better business owner but also a better person holding me accountable to my own advice.

3. What gets measure gets improved

Knowing how the different areas of your business are performing can help you to evaluate where your business is strong, where it is weaker and factors you can change to help it improve. There are many businesses owners who may not have even re-assessed their business's plan since the day they launched, or there are other more established businesses that know that their business is slowing down, but they do not know why.

In the last deep recession the UK had after the 2007 crash, most business owners would blame the economy, but many of them would have not revisited key areas of performance in their business, simply because they were not measuring it.

It is this reason that moving through Brexit as a business owner, you should focus on specific factors that are easy to measure and show the areas where your business is successful or in need of improvement when compared to the rest of the market.

These are known as key performance indicators (KPIs).

During Brexit it is vital to measure both non-financial targets as well as financial ones. All businesses are different but below are some areas to consider (in no particular order):

- Your customers - eg how many you have, how often they use you and how many customers you have lost or gained

- Customer service - eg waiting times for assistance, complaints, or reasons customers have complained

- Market share - eg whether your share of the market increased or decreased against competitors

- Your staff - eg satisfaction levels, work quality or attendance records

The benefits of measuring KPI's

Your strategic visions can sometimes be difficult to communicate, but you can break your main objectives down into smaller targets to make it easier to manage.

By doing this, your smaller targets become more like day-to-day operations which, once completed, move you closer to your final goal.

Whether your performance improvement goals are related to marketing, sales, customer service, profit or any aspect of business for that matter, choosing the proper key performance indicators (KPIs) to focus on is the first step towards measurable improvement.

As Peter Drucker (Austrian-born American management consultant, educator and author) once said…

"What gets measured gets improved."

I love this principle because it is easy to understand that by simply examining an activity regularly, fundamentally changes the activity by forcing you to pay attention to it.

It becomes 'a thing' and therefore if you can quantify your current performance you can then begin to measure how 'things' are improving, or diminishing, over a period of time.

Choosing the right KPIs to focus on during Brexit

When the sea upon which you are sailing is rocking, you have to retrench to the core objectives and principle of your businesses.

It may be best to focus on what you do best and not all the side projects and distractions that 'the good times' afford you.

My advice for Brexitpreneurs is to choose KPIs that are directly related to your primary business goals.

For example, Mark Hayes, Shopify's (global ecommerce software giant) Director of Communications, provides the following examples of common ecommerce goals and related KPIs.

Goal 1 – Boost sales 10% in the next quarter. KPIs include daily sales, conversion rate and site traffic

Goal 2 – Increase conversion rate 2% in the next year. KPIs

include conversion rate, shopping cart abandonment rate, associated shipping rate trends, competitive price trends.

Goal 3 – Grow site traffic 20% in the next year. KPIs include site traffic, traffic sources, promotional click-through rates, social shares, bounce rates.

Goal 4 – Reduce customer service calls by half in the next 6 months. KPIs include service call satisfaction, identify of page visited immediately before the call, event that lead to the call.

As you can see, each of the potential KPIs listed in the four examples are directly related to the core business goal.

For my business Yomp Marketing, a client services business, we have set the following goals:

Goal 1 – Maintain funnel 90 – 20 – 5. These numbers are based upon our funnel and our 'client on-boarding' capacity. For every 90 leads we get, we have 20 meaningful conversations which we vet the clients to only take on 5 new clients a month, as this is the capacity we can handle for our core lead generation product.

Goal 2 – Increase average client value to £2,500 p/m. Because of the quality of our work and time we put into each client, plus our self-imposed limitations on capacity to maintain that quality we therefore target ourselves upon moving our average from £2k p/m to £2.5k p/m.

Goal 3 – Increase client retention rate by 10%. All companies lose clients and we are proud to say that we have a very high client retention rate, but we want to focus on the small bits that all add up to longer client retentions.

You should also only focus on a few key metrics, rather than 100's of data points. One of the things I love about my industry (Digital Marketing) is that you can measure everything with very detailed metrics, such as views, clicks, conversions, opens, sends, the list goes on and is sometimes too detailed and distracts you from the most important drivers of business growth.

As you begin to identify KPIs for your business you should be aware that less is almost always more. Rather than choosing dozens of metrics to measure and report on you should focus on just a few key metrics.

As you can imagine, every company, industry and business model is very different so it is difficult to pinpoint an exact number for the amount of KPIs you should have. Although, based on my experience, in most cases you should aim to identify somewhere between three and ten KPIs.

As a Brexitpreneur, knowing your numbers is vital and through KPI's you will understand what is going well and what needs improving, there has never been a more important time to know these numbers.

4. Brand Britain

What does Brand Britain stand for today and how can we take advantage of it?

To get to grips with what the world perceives of Brand Britain we need to look at the trends of the past.

Britain is a brand constantly in flux, from the picture-perfect moments of the London 2012 Olympics, the swinging sixties, the Global uncertainty of the Falklands Conflict, the 'Cool Britannia' of the 90's, the 'loads of money' 80's, to an ongoing fascination with the Royal family, and now Brexit.

'Cool Britannia', a pun on the title of the British patriotic song 'Rule Britannia', was a period of increased pride in the culture of the United Kingdom throughout most of the 1990's. It was the success of Britpop and musical acts such as the Spice Girls and Oasis which led to a renewed feeling of optimism in the United Kingdom following the uncertain Brand Britain years of the Thatcher lead 1980s with the Falklands War and wide spread industrial strikes and privatisation of many nationalised industries.

Efforts again to boost Brand Britain are coming thick and fast as the government and industry seek to make use of our national identity to push on beyond Brexit.

The £100m 'GREAT Britain' campaign, a cross-government

initiative promoting the UK as a place to visit, study and do business, is still showcasing the best of what the UK has to offer to inspire the world and encourage people to visit, do business, invest and study in the UK.

It is the Government's most ambitious international promotional campaign ever, uniting the efforts of the public and private sector to generate jobs and growth for Britain.

It says that:

The UK has a huge amount to offer, with world-class universities, ground breaking research, high tech start-ups and entrepreneurial business people.

We are global leaders in the creative industries like music, fashion, design and film.

We can offer visitors unforgettable experiences, breath-taking landscapes and iconic attractions.

The campaigns aim is to encourage people around the world to think and feel differently about modern Britain.

Leading up to the Brexit vote in 2015 Britain has enjoyed a further renaissance in recent years with an outpouring of public spirit linked to the Royal family for the wedding of the Duke and Duchess of Cambridge, the Queen's diamond jubilee and the birth of Prince George and Princess Charlotte.

Moreover, many saw an inspiring picture of what it means to be British in the opening ceremony of the London 2012 Olympics.

But in a post Brexit world, do the Royal family and sporting events have enough Brand Britain leverage to drive forward global opinion that Britain is back on track after the uncertainty of the leave vote?

Zaid Al-Zaidy, chief executive of marketing agency Above and Beyond, believes that attaching British values to a brand is no longer enough.

Research carried out within his agency and among its clients shows few would buy goods solely because they are British.

"People want a sense of belonging, participation and shared hopes. Today we live in an 'experience society' – the only products that survive are the ones that fulfil a need and deliver a service really well"

he says. *"We judge brands by what they do for me, rather than what they say they do."*

So, promotion of Brand Britain needs to avoid the simplistic stereotypes of Big Ben and red buses and instead look more at the experience people have of Britain.

Al-Zaidy suggests looking at Brand Britain as a source of inspiration for world events.

"Britain is like a petri dish for innovation – such as Framestore's special-effects work in the film Gravity. There's a real sense that the UK is the incubator for great things that happen globally – you can pass through Britain and see history in the making,"

Al-Zaidy makes an extremely interesting point, as a Brexitpreneur you need to harness that sense of history and pride in Brand Britain if that is the route you decided to take. If you do, you have to deliver on it, you have to be Brand Britain, not just add it as a marketing ploy.

Brexit proves people want a sense of belonging and pride. That is what national identity allows them to have and in some way, was the asset the leave campaign used best to win the vote.

Although we belonged to the EU the general consensus even for remainders was that we were not 100% proud of it. We were however proud to be British and that feeling is only going to grow as we pull together to handle Brexit.

Millions of people made the decision to leave, so the opportunity is as high as ever within the UK for Brand Britain.

People are simply looking for reasons to engage with British products and services because of the value they give to the British economy, not because they have a Union Jack on it.

It is in our culture to 'do our bit' and this core British saying that dates back to the 1st World War and beyond should not be underestimated.

The Brexit consumer economy will now look for real British spirit and values from its suppliers and not the hyper inflated foreign versions of Brand Britain.

Will this mean that clothing manufactures such as Ralph Lauren who has tried to do British better than the British for years and in many cases, has been extremely successful at it, starts to see a decline in the UK market with consumers selecting authentic British brand stories over foreign 'trying to be British' imports?

The Future of Brexit Brand Britain Globally

Britain has an identity that has always made it seem slightly detached from Europe. This is partly geographical, partly political and partly historical but is entirely unavoidable. Whereas countries such as Germany, France and Spain have always been 'European' I have never come across a consensus that Britain was also 'European' in a cultural and societal sense.

Many experts say that Brexit will mean one of only two options. Britain can either brand itself as an individual international player or it can revert to colonial favouritism.

In my opinion, it is a mix of the two, I do feel that the low hanging fruit for our new outward looking global economy will be through English speaking countries, it was unsurprising that only days after Brexit, Australia and New Zealand were at the negotiating table.

But has the damage already been done with these old trading allies? When joining the EU, Britain toned down many of its trade relations with former colonial powers such as Canada, South Africa, Australia and New Zealand.

Some of these countries may be willing to open up their arms to Britain, seeking favourable trading agreements with familiar partners, but others may be seeking to bolster agreements made since the heyday of Britain as an independent powerhouse. As an example, back in 1955 Britain took in over 65% of New Zealand's exports, today Britain counts for less than 5%. There is certainly room for this to grow, therefore New Zealand and others like it have plenty to gain from us, as well as what we can offer them.

On the other hand, as an individual international entity, we have the scope to grow relations with the United States, South America and Asian markets with almost boundless potential.

Our negotiators and industry leaders have great opportunities in other countries and continents. The mere fact that we will be looking at faster time lines and have a new vigour to bring to the negotiating table, will be a catalyst for change.

You also may find this for your business, be open to all enquiries globally and do put feelers out to all markets if they are appropriate. Britain is on the radar and fellow entrepreneurs in foreign economies will want to quickly take advantage of this outward looking ethos to see if there is business to be done.

Either way brand Britain has a lot of work to do post Brexit.

A Remain result would have meant that Brand Britain fulfilled its stereotype as a solid, predictable, rock of a country, but now business leaders will have to realise that even one of the most traditional brands in the world has the potential to shock and surprise.

For business short term, instability is a weakness, the markets do not like it. Long term, we can shape our own stability without being connected to a potentially unsteady Europe.

5. Think Globally

I heard David Cameron speak pre-vote at a conference in London and he said:

"Currently 1 in 5 UK businesses export globally. If that increased to 1 in 4, we would wipe out our deficit."

That is a pretty powerful thought!

Aside from doing your bit for the country, the business world has changed so much with the advances of technology, that it is a distinct possibility for all small businesses.

Look at the statistics:

Facebook founded in 2004 and in less than 10 years has a turnover of $100 billion.

Alibaba founded in 1999 and now a turnover of $12 billion.

You might not want to be a billion-pound company but if you are ambitious and want to grow quickly you should look at the global market.

Certainly, SME sized businesses based elsewhere in the world are looking to capture the UK market as part of their growth strategy.

As a Brexitpreneur, you'll know that there's already massive change in the markets. Change is inevitable, but as a country you simply do not turn off the taps, similarly the EU nations are still going to want to export to the UK and it is therefore in everyone's interest to make this as simple as possible for the businesses leaders to keep trading.

Start Selling Internationally

If you have a product or service that is selling well in the UK, then there will almost certainly be a demand for it internationally.

The UK accounts for just 1/20th of the world's economy, so confining your business to the domestic market is overlooking a huge potential.

I do understand that for many SME's there are countless reasons why you might not be exporting.

You simply might be happy with how businesses is going domestically and you do not want to complicate things by looking abroad.

I certainly empathise with the initial thought process that you don't want to deal with the perceived hassle of regulations, red tape, paperwork and cultural barriers. Other business owners who I have interviewed have seen exporting is a risky venture especially in these uncertain Brexit times. Even for the most ambitious entrepreneurs I meet, they still are a bit confused upon where to start.

Each of these concerns is a misconception.

Exporting actually reduces risk by spreading it across a wider range of customers and protecting your business if the UK demand for your product or service falls.

Selling into other countries will also give you kudos from a branding perspective and a far better feel for your product or service from a research point of view.

There is nothing like multiple international markets to help you shape and improve what you sell from an operation basis and for the product/serve itself, all of which will have a positive effect on your domestic sales and a far more robust business.

Which Country to start with?

Research from the Department of International Trade (DIT) suggests that one in three exporters don't know which market to target.

For entrepreneurs looking to start researching into the viability of exporting, I would suggest looking into markets geographically close but also where English is a commonly used second language, for example Sweden, Denmark, Belgium and the Netherlands.

One of the first business trips I remember going on with my father when my brother, sister and I were kids was to the Netherlands. I asked him at the time why he was doing business in Holland, and aside from the business case for that particular opportunity, he said that the Dutch "share our humour" which as simple as it sounds, is as profound as language itself.

It was Robert Orben an American magician and professional comedy writer, who famously said:

"If you can laugh together, you can work together."

I believe that humour is totally underestimated in business, it has been a foundation for all relationships I have built and the strongest still have a light-hearted element of fun sitting front and centre of every meeting I have.

My father (like Tim and I) built his business with his brother, Nigel. They did deals all over Europe and Nigel's humour was notorious.

It was sometimes a bit worrying, one famous occasion, was in a meeting with potential Dutch partners who had flown over that morning and were meeting with Dennis and Nigel for the very first time.

Sitting in the meeting Nigel had asked them how their flight was, which they said was good, he then asked what aeroplane they took, they said it was a 'Fokker' (a Dutch aircraft manufacturer named after its founder, Anthony Fokker) – Nigel immediately replied saying "would it not start then!"

An off the cuff slice of British humour which could have insulted the recipients, yet it was greeted with laughter, the Dutch guys having appreciated the joke.

This broke the ice and the meeting went on to conclude a very successful deal!

Sometimes humour is as important as language when building international relationships, although Dennis regularly warned Nigel that his comment may not have worked so well with the Germans clients they have, as the Dutch do have a very similar sense of humour to the Brits.

Sometimes humour is as important as language when building international relationships.

Further from home you could look to the Gulf as there are frequent daily flights to Dubai, Abu Dhabi, Bahrain, Qatar and other countries in that region.

The USA continues to buy more UK exports than any other country. When considering doing business in America it is important to be aware that while it offers huge potential it can also be a challenging, highly regulated market for new exporters.

When you're ready you need to make a decision as to which part of the USA will be your initial focus. It could be a city, state or even a region: the east coast, mid-west, west coast.

Using a small area of this huge market as a starter or pilot could prove the most successful strategy.

My advice is to think about the English-speaking countries; they have proven to be the first people that we are negotiating with outside of the EU.

If we can do trade deals with Australia to export our services, as well as our products, at a lower tax importation rate, then we will find ourselves in an impressive position to grow internationally.

Personally, I have sold into the Irish and Scandinavian markets in the past with my product design businesses, my lead generation business has clients in Ireland, the USA, Australia and New Zealand. I am now looking to turn the volume up on those territories because of Brexit, not despite of Brexit.

4 steps to help a small business expand globally

As a quick step by step guide to get you started I have the following core pieces of advice for any small business looking to expand globally:

1. **Engage with Department for International Trade (DIT) Trade Missions:**

   This is high level stuff but it opens doors that you would have never been able to achieve on your own. Use Brand Britain and I suggest seeking out a trade mission that is specific to your industry: be it health, food, automotive, technology etc.

The DIT run many events in the year and are always available to discuss the possibility of working with globally looking small businesses.

As a Brexitpreneur you should be think about your angle and of course make use of all the funding that Government will be throwing at businesses who want to export post Brexit.

2. **Build a Network:**
Just as you would in the UK, attend networking events with other organisations already exporting to or thinking about exporting to your target market. You learn as much by hearing what not to do as what to do.

Those contacts are invaluable and as well as DIT there are a range of forums and membership organisations linking countries and markets

3. **Attract foreign buyers to your website:**
An excellent way of determining if you are ready to go global is the level of foreign activity on your website and other marketing channels. To do this you must participate in and be active on as many of the top social media platforms as possible for foreign buyers to find your site.

Attracting paying customers requires that you develop a relationship with them, gain their trust, and offer products/services they want.

You won't be able to foster online success with Instagram alone, for example. That's a good start, but you must support it with a Twitter, Facebook, Linked In, Pinterest and even Snapchat presence.

Putting all the social platforms to work together creates a winning online strategy, provided you stick to a topic or theme for which you are knowledgeable and adds value to you audience.

Your goal should be to create a big picture view of what you are trying to accomplish with your export business, and then make sure the right message gets in front of the right people at the right time.

If it does your traffic analytics will show you this and it will be a good indicator of if you are going to be successful overseas.

4. **Get started:**
When I was last at Heathrow airport all along the walls are HSBC's billboards about international travel and

international businesses. One of the messages on the wall was very fitting, it said:

"In the future, even the smallest business will be multinational."

Another showed a price board at a kid's lemonade stand marked up in dollars, euros and yen. It said

"Now any small business can be a global business".

One of my mentors, Daniel Priestly talks about 'Global Small Businesses' in his bestselling book The Entrepreneur Revolution. The world is talking global so now is the time to think beyond localities and get started.

The global small business and international entrepreneur revolution is happening, regardless of whether we are in the EU or not.

It is happening all around the world we need to raise our vision outwardly from Europe to previously far away markets of South America, Asia, and Australasia who are preparing themselves for working with our post Brexit businesses. So why not get out there and fly the flag for your British business.

6. Innovate, Innovate, Innovate

Innovation is such a key asset for any growing business, even if you are in the most traditional of industry sectors you have to innovate, innovate, innovate.

Going into Brexit we will see large brands that have been built by entrepreneurial owners, but through managerial changes, usually following flotation on the stock markets or a large capital purchase from professional investors, finding themselves being run by lawyers and accountants.

When the economy starts to head into rocky seas, there is just not the culture of innovation within these businesses to re-invent their offering and transform out of trouble.

Take the last financial crisis Britain went through, we lost a whole wave of household names, who were not able to innovate out of trouble and have subsequently been sold for rock bottom prices to innovative companies, or have ceased to exist:

Blockbuster, Comet, Goldman Sachs, JJB Sports, Phones 4U, Clinton Cards, Game, Borders, Barratts, Alexon, T J Hughes, Jane Norman, Habitat, Focus DIY, Floors-2-Go, the Officers Club, Oddbins, Ethel Austin, Faith Shoes, Adams Childrenswear, Thirst Quench, Stylo, Mosaic, Principles, Sofa Workshop, Allied Carpets, Viyella, Dewhurst, Woolworths, MFI, and Zavvi/Virgin Megastore.

If you look through that list there is not many seismic shifts that has disrupted our buying behaviour, after all we do still wear clothes, buy kitchens, install new floors and sit on sofas.

Even for obviously affected industries like video rental, it is true that our buying behaviour has shifted to watching movies and box set videos on demand through digital platforms like Netflix's. But as a global economy we do still spend a fortune on home entertainment.

As a case study let's look at Netflix vs Blockbuster.

Netflix was founded in 1997 during Blockbuster's heyday and the company grew by starting in the DVD by mail business.

In fact, in 2000 they did offer themselves for sale to Blockbuster for $50 million, but Blockbuster declined the offer.

Seven year later in 2007, Netflix expanded their business with the introduction of streaming media, as well as retaining the DVD and Blu-Ray rental service. They saw the opportunity of the internet and jumped on it.

Blockbuster who had massive reach and a vast client base were too distracted by needing to keep their high street shops open and their staff employed that they did not innovate at the right time.

They were the right company at the right time but lacked foresight and that ruthless edge to cut away the 'video store' model and go all in on digital rentals/subscription.

Now Netflix serves over 190 countries and in 2013 it introduced itself into the film and television industry with its first series; House of Cards.

At its peak in 2004, Blockbuster had 60,000 employees and 9,000 stores worldwide with a market value of $5 billion and revenues of $5.9 billion

For the year ending 2015, Netflix only have 3,100 employees, a market value of just under $29 billion and revenues of $6.77 billion.

This is the landscape that the internet brings, it is a global economy where serving 190 countries with just over 3,000 staff is totally achievable.

In fact, if you take away the latest innovation by Netflix into film and series creation and just looked at their distribution and subscriber service you can halve that head count and still be able to serve all those countries at the same top line revenue figures, because making movies just helps their bottom line, not turnover.

Not being part of the EU has not hampered Netflix's growth, neither did it put Blockbuster out of business, seeing opportunities and innovating into it was the winner of the day between the two companies.

If you ask Netflix, they were delighted to see such upheaval in an industry that they operated in since 2007, they did after all desire to be part of Blockbuster at one point, but when their sea got rocky, they switched ship, Blockbuster tried too late and was too heavily weighed down by their head count and stores, they simply could not make it to shore.

The question is why? The answer to that question for 90% of businesses that go into administration is that it comes down to one thing: lack of innovation.

My theory is simple: for every problem that a large company has, there is a start up somewhere working on that problem, it is just a matter of finding that team and working with them or if you ignore them more often than not they tend to out-innovate the incumbents. The above story of Netflix VS Blockbuster is a clear example of this phenomena.

Large companies have known this for a while and they are worried, perhaps that is why the mantra of, 'if you can't beat them buy them' has been successful.

For large companies needing to work through Brexit, mergers and acquisitions can be the solution to solve issues of scale and innovation but as HP showed us with the acquisition of Autonomy, success isn't always guaranteed.

On the other hand Mark Zuckerberg realised that he was so late in the mobile space that he spent $1Billion on Instagram (now worth $35Billion) and the most legendary deal so far from Facebook was WhatsApp for $19Billion consequently he now dominates social on all important verticals.

For the Brexitpreneur you may well have the opportunity to be bought by a larger company if you have found your niche and you are solving meaningful problems through innovation.

In every industry I see this opportunity and so ask yourself a simple question:

How can I innovate and become the next Netflix, Uber, Spotify, Shazam, Tesla, Tinder, SnapChat, Nest or Dyson?

Now may well be the best time to do so.

7. Demonstrate thought leadership

Business growth can be enabled in many ways, yet most business owners focus on the traditional ways such as more sales, new products, new markets, new brands, mergers and acquisitions etc.

What many businesses don't seem to value and/or understand is the power of knowledge sharing.

With Brexit, we are all being challenged to deal with change in every aspect of our business and no one has all of the answers that the fast moving global market will present us with.

This represents a unique opportunity for Brexitpreneurs to share their unique knowledge and understanding of their industry.

Begin to assess, package and share your own best practices, strategic knowledge, case studies and results to fuel business growth.

Beyond business growth, thought leadership can fuel growth and opportunities for employee engagement and infuse excitement back into a workplace culture. Employees want their leaders to be more vocal in sharing their perspectives about the future. They want leaders that are proactive about informing them of what's upon the horizon so they can prepare themselves for what's next and contribute in more meaningful and purposeful ways.

To win from Brexit, you need to demonstrate your thought leadership.

You need to publish the ideas that you have.

When you start sharing your options and helping others you start to become an Industry leader, 'an Influencer'.

Jane Frankland is an excellent example of this, having run, then recently sold, her Cyber Security businesses, she now shares her thoughts on leadership in the Cyber Security sphere and specifically the lack of female representation in the industry. Through doing this she is now recognised as one of the 'go to' people in the industry.

She recently commented on social media that:

"Last week IBM invited me to Wimbledon (Grand slam Tennis Tournament) as their special guest.

One of their Distinguished Engineers & CTOs looked after me, I had a tour of the Broadcasting Centre and saw the tennis play on Court 1.

The reason I was invited was because I've been identified as a TOP Influencer in my market (UK cyber security). IBM commissioned an independent agency to assess the market and now want to forge strong relationships with market influencers.

This is pretty pioneering and I believe the shape of things to come. I believe being a KPI (Key Person of Influence) is going to be increasingly important as we see "influence" become more measured via technology."

In response to this Carmina Lees, Director of IBM's Security Business Unit, UK & Ireland says:

"The opinions of top influencers in our target market is very important. They are seen as trusted advisors in the marketplace. Having a strategy and establishing a dialogue with top influencers allows us to demonstrate what IBM can offer our clients and raise our profile in the market."

The above example demonstrates a typical win / win between big businesses and industry influencers. After Brexit there will be many businesses in the EU and also in Britain looking for the leading voices with opinions and experience they respect. Just as in other walks of life you have to go out there and earn that respect.

You need to be the entrepreneur that walks tallest across all of your industry. You need to claim your sector.

If you're an accountant, be the go-to accountant for information on Brexit, on how Brexit impacts your clients, how should businesses account better for Brexit.

If you're a solicitor, be the go-to person for how the law is going to change, how the government is shaping the laws left open after exiting the EU and how that impacts your clients, or industry and the wider economy.

If you're a landscape gardener, talk about how the impact of Brexit will shape landscape gardening, how there is less red tape for certain gardening practices or how with an uncertain property market people are moving less and therefore investing in the properties they live in, investing in better gardens and value added areas in gardens such as outside offices to accommodate more room as people are not moving home as much as they used to.

In uncertain times, people are hungry for information, people need thought leadership.

8. Negotiate and Do Deals

Do you sometimes have the feeling that you could have got a better deal when buying or selling? If so, you are not alone, as there is almost always a better deal to be had.

With the whole country looking to do deals internally and internationally, the Brexitpreneur needs to gear him/herself up for doing better and more frequent deals.

When I was on the BBC's television show 'The Apprentice' I managed to lead my team to the highest ever deal values ever seen on the show in its entire 13 years of existence.

We sold £4.2 million pounds' worth of 1 and 2 bedroom flats, off plan, in 8 hours.

I was also proud to be my season's highest billing candidate, making me the best deal maker in 13 series.

I have a passion for sales, but I am never pushy, in fact I am more fun, informative and personable.

It is my job as a deal maker to look after everyone's interests; if done correctly there is always a great deal to find.

When I do deals I always adopt the same five principles, regardless of whether I am buying or selling:

1. **A better deal for you doesn't have to mean a worse deal for them**

   Work to the basis that there is a deal to be uncovered that is better for both parties - a 'I win and you win' deal. Your job is to find that win / win each and every time.

2. **Make sure you understand and explore the other side's situation and pressures**

   Does it help him/her if you buy this week instead of next, have it in blue not green, arrange delivery yourself, and pay now instead of 30 days? Explore all the options that you can think of.

3. **Develop add-on's or parts of the deal you can trade**

   Work out in advance what aspects of the deal are essential for you and which you can play with, together with the value of those add-ons to you. Do you need that 'free' printer with the PC? Their value may well be very different to the other party.

4. **Know your absolute bottom line**

   You MUST work out in advance where your bottom line is and be prepared to walk away from the deal if it doesn't at least meet it - just knowing this yourself will give you the confidence, body language and tone of voice that will in itself translate into better deals.

5. **The biggest deal may not be this one**

   You will find that applying these ideas will improve the feeling and the 'win / win' nature of your deals. If both parties walk away happier then this is the best basis for building long lasting business relationships. In the long run this will mean more deals from this one relationship in the future, plus they may also tell their friends.

In the new post Brexit world, the deal makers will help to win the day, keep your eye out for them whenever you can.

If you are not a natural, learn the skills but also look to align yourself with a natural deal maker and harness their abilities to progress your business.

9. Use Government incentives

During this time of uncertainty, the government will be seriously looking to support small businesses in as many ways as they can.

Unfortunately, as an organisation the Government are not always the best at reaching out to small businesses. This creates both a problem but also an opportunity.

The problem for you is finding the time to educate yourself on what works and what is appropriate in terms of incentives and grants for your business.

The opportunity is that most businesses do not get their act together and leave so much funding on the table that there is usually a budget for excess, which makes winning grants and obtaining incentives relatively easy if you know what you are doing.

The government breaks down their finance and support for your business page on their Gov.uk website as follows:

1. Grants
2. Finance and loans
3. Business support e.g. mentoring, consultancy
4. Funding for small and medium-sized businesses, plus start-ups

Of the above categories, there are currently 531 schemes, of which some are national such as the Apprenticeship Scheme and some are local, such as SMART: SCOTLAND - which is an incentive supporting research and development projects in small Scottish companies.

The Gov.uk website does have a post code filtering device that will offer a number of government incentives based upon your geographic area.

In my area, Surrey, identified as 'South East', there are 49 schemes that my business has access to, fewer schemes than if I was in the North East, for example, where there are 51.

However there are many funding, grant and advisory schemes to help businesses grow locally, nationally and internationally.

I would recommend if you are looking to grow or get advice, I would do the following:

1. On a local level contact your local enterprise partnership (LEP)

2. On an International level contact the Department for International Trade (DIT)

The above can become confusing (too many abbreviations for my liking!), so I have split out the following explanations:

Local Enterprise Partnerships (LEPs)

In England, local enterprise partnerships (LEPs) are voluntary partnerships between local authorities and businesses. The LEP's were set up in 2011 by the Department for Business, Innovation and Skills to help determine local economic priorities and lead economic growth and job creation within the local area.

They carry out some of the functions previously carried out by the regional development agencies which were abolished in March 2012. To date there are 39 local enterprise partnerships in operation.

I have found working with my LEP very easy, they are after all there to help you access funding to grow your businesses within the local economy. They will become more and more relevant in the post-Brexit era.

Some of the funding for the LEP's did come from the European Structural and Investment Funding pot.

In fact, my LEP did have €50m for the financial year 2015/16. However, this money should still be available to the LEP's through redistribution post-Brexit by the UK government and it probably allows for more freedom of use by the LEP's as they will not have Brussels guiding them on how to use it.

It is my belief that post-Brexit access to this funding through LEP's will be far easier.

To give you a few examples of some of the activities an LEP conducts my local LEP, Enterprise M3 for 2015/16:

- A successful application for a new Enterprise Zone for the Enterprise M3 area, covering three sites at Basing View, Basingstoke, Longcross Park near Chertsey, and Whitehill & Bordon in East Hampshire.

  Enterprise Zones are designated areas across England that provide tax breaks and Government support. They are great places to do business especially for both new and expanding firms

- The launch of the Enterprise M3 Growth Hub, which provides expert advice and resource network to businesses with high innovation and growth potential to achieve results quickly through a personal, tailored service focused on Growth

- Supporting businesses to engage with cutting-edge 5G technology through an initial £1.75m investment in the 5G Innovation Centre at the University of Surrey

- Prioritising the delivery of new homes across our Local Growth Fund programme, which as a whole has the potential to unlock up to 24,000 homes

- Working with partners across the private and public sector to update our intelligence on the commercial property market in Enterprise M3

- Works beginning onsite for four new Science, Technology, Engineering and Maths (STEM) Skills Centres funded from our Local Growth Fund

- Launching the first round of grants to support SMEs as part of the development of a Woodfuel Hub Network

In my opinion the requirement for a greater use and level of funding into the LEP will grow in the Brexit economy, as Brexitpreneurs we should be using and gaining as much funding as we can from schemes offered by LEP's.

Department for International Trade (DIT)

UK Trade and Investment (DIT) is a Government department working with businesses based in the United Kingdom to ensure their success in international markets, and encourage the best overseas companies to look to the UK as their global partner of choice. Their services are provided in over 100 markets throughout the world.

Their services are delivered to businesses by:

- Over 1,200 staff outside the UK
- Over 500 staff in our London and Glasgow headquarters
- Over 400 staff based in the English regions

Which clearly shows the commitment by the UK government to grow exports.

DIT Export services for UK businesses

The Government understands that in the Brexit era, Trade and Investment has never been more important to the country's economic prospects.

As Brexitpreneurs we need to use DIT, its sole purpose is to help British companies of all sizes to grow their business through international trade by offering expert advice and practical support through a range of programmes. It also connects businesses to the world's top commercial opportunities and drives targeted campaigns centred on them.

They split this help into the following areas:

Events and Missions

Events are one of the most effective ways to support companies that are looking for trade opportunities and that are undergoing periods of transition. The DIT calendar of events has some 400 core events and missions, and 1000 opportunities across TAP "Trade Access Programme" and the English National Regions.

DIT Events Portal

The DIT Events Portal provides a single calendar view of all DIT Events and Missions, and has been developed to provide companies with more detailed information on each event in order to help them decide on the most appropriate event to attend. The calendar can be filtered and searched by sector and/or market.

There are also detailed events websites which include more information about the event and also allow users to register for an event.

Business Opportunities

The DIT Business Opportunities service is a web based system that allows UK companies to register for 1,000's of free sales leads in 42 sectors in over 100 countries. These are sourced by DIT experts and put you in touch with companies in that market who are looking to source millions of pounds worth of goods and services from the UK.

Webinar

The DIT Webinar service runs hundreds of free hour long internet events covering topics, sectors and countries around the world, helping you shape your export plan.

These events allow you to interact with the experts in specific sectors and countries and allow you to ask questions to enhance your knowledge.

Open to Export

Open to Export is DIT's free, online advice service for UK companies looking to grow internationally. It offers free information and support on anything to do with exporting and hosts online discussions via its forum, webinars and social media where businesses can ask any export question, and learn from each other.

The DIT will play an important pre and post Brexit role, so do get involved with it.

10. Celebrate the Success of your Customers

Trust is going to be a major factor when organisations are looking for new suppliers in this rocky economic environment. You also need to make sure you understand your current customers and make them into raving fans of your brand.

There is no better way to do this than to collect case studies and recommendations.

They can be as short as a picture and a quick testimonial or they can be multi-page articles where you dive into someone's story, problems, and solutions.

They are important because it's not enough to say that you have the best product or service. You have to show proof. People want to see that others like them have found success with your company.

Testimonials and word of mouth are the driving force behind 20 - 50% of all purchasing decisions and yet only about one third of businesses are actively seeking and collecting customer reviews on an ongoing basis.

If you're not investing in testimonials right now, you need to start ASAP.

Recent behavioural research by Granify (US eCommerce Software) revealed that 'social proof' is often more important to online buyers than 'low prices' when influencing purchasing decisions.

An excerpt from the McKinsey (Global Management Consulting Firm) Quarterly report states:

"...*consumers overwhelmed by product choices tune out the ever-growing barrage of traditional marketing, word of mouth cuts through the noise quickly and effectively.*

...Its influence is greatest when consumers are buying a product for the first time or when products are relatively expensive, factors that tend to make people conduct more research, seek more opinions, and deliberate longer than they otherwise would."

Now consider that in Google's *Zero Moment Of Truth* report, they found that the average buyer in 2011 used 10.4 sources of information before buying.

Can you guess which of the 10.4 sources buyers found most influential?

According to an article in Econsultancy, when a site has customer reviews, 63% of visitors are more likely to make a purchase and reviews produce an average of 18% uplift in sales.

The online video review site EXPO found that customer reviews are twelve times more trusted than descriptions that come from manufacturers.

To see just how powerful testimonials can be in action, let's look at WikiJob, one of the UK's largest graduate job sites.

They conducted a test between two web pages, where they only added three testimonials to a test page to compete against their original version.

The testimonials where as follows:

"Good training for the work environment in Europe."

"Very useful for practice!"

"Almost a carbon copy for the real aptitude test."

Notice that the testimonials do not even include names or a source and aren't over the top by any means.

However, Version B, the test page still surprisingly increased WikiJob's conversions by an impressive 34%. Can you imagine what that would do to your business to get 34% more leads?

When all is said and done, testimonials are really just affirmations for your customer to validate or solidify their feelings on a future purchase.

By putting testimonials and reviews where they're expected, making sure they speak to your buyer's persona and prompting them at the right time, you put yourself one step closer to winning at Brexit.

11. Be relentless.

Being relentless is all about consistently and thoroughly pushing out your ideas, your brand and your business, over and over and over again.

Not the same message and not always on the same platform, but just consistently being there, being that, blog, that tweet, that YouTube video, that Facebook post, that email campaign, that sponsorship of a local business event.

This simple strategy could be critical to your growth post-Brexit as it reminds the world regularly, that you are here and very ready for business.

Market research continuously proves the obvious: a person needs to know you, your reputation, and your product or service before he/she is willing to make a purchase.

How many touches are required on average before the sale?

Building visibility, familiarity and a positive reputation takes time and a series of memorable contacts. How many contacts (or "touches") it takes depends on many factors, such as price, complexity of product, "need versus want," competition, etc. But the truth is, the sales process is exactly that – a process.

In the case of an impulse purchase, only one contact is needed, but this usually happens inside a favourite store where there is already a level of confidence and trust, or the price is so low that it does not matter to the buyer.

For non-impulse purchases, a good starting point for thinking about becoming relentless is the 'Rule of Seven,' formulated by marketing expert Dr Jeffrey Lant.

Lant states that to penetrate the buyer's consciousness and make significant penetration in a given market, you have to contact the prospect a minimum of seven times within an 18-month period.

As the internet expands and the barrage of messages we all receive increases I would suggest that this rule is tweaked upwards a few touches. In fact, as a Brexitpreneur you should always be thinking ahead of the market and trying to improve on every trend.

For my market and the clients I work with, we believe it is far higher, from the average we are seeing across all the products and services we promote it is more like 22 touches.

That is 22 times a potential client has to see your brand, read your stuff, engage with your team, see you and hear about you.

This also has to be across multiple platforms, because if people are just seeing your brand on Facebook, there may be a credibility issue with being 'the bloke who talks about accountancy on Facebook', for example.

If people only see you on YouTube, they might think, "Who's this? - They just fancy themselves as a bit of a YouTube personality".

But if you can go out across multiple platforms and engaging on and off line with your target audience demonstrating your excellent product and clear thought leadership, you will become relentless: a steady stream of sales could start being generated.

To demonstrate how the 22 touches work, below is an example for a product based company:

1. A potential customer sees your product for the first time at a trade show where you are exhibiting.

2. They take a flyer you have given them, which soon finds the floor or a bin.

3. They notice your ad on Facebook a few weeks later but don't decide to click.

4. They spot a friend using the product and ask if your product works as advertised.

5. They decide to click on your Facebook page to see what kind of stuff you post after a friend shares your status.

6. They catch a friend mentioning your brand in a Twitter contest they've decided to enter for a chance to win your product.

7. They like your Facebook page and see a post from you every few days.

8. The next week, they see a stranger with your product at the park.

9. They are online and a banner ad for your brand is on the right hand column of a website, they do not click on it.

10. The next day they see a friend using the product on snapchat.

11. They visit your website and read the reviews.

12. Later they see your re-targeting ad and decide click on it and submit their email to receive a coupon.

13. They find your coupon in their junk folder and delete it.

14. They receive a thought leadership email from you about the product and scan it quickly, reading 35% of the information.

15. They receive an email reminder about the 1st coupon a week later and decide to visit your site (but abandon the cart when they see they have to pay shipping).

16. They receive an email with a link to a series of YouTube videos on the product and subscribe to the channel.

17. As a subscriber the next week they get an update with a new video you have put on YouTube channel and the click on it to watch.

18. Another friend is seen using the product on Twitter.

19. They see a new 2nd coupon for free shipping in their email.

20. They make a note to buy, but get distracted by cat videos.

21. They get the 2nd Coupons reminder email and click on it.

22. They finally buy your product from your site!

The above is a long list of touches, but I am sure you would have found many of the stages familiar when making decisions. Many businesses simply are not sufficiently relentless with their messaging and communication and consequently lose opportunities.

My Final Thoughts

Brexit has and will continue to create massive disruption in our politics, press and economy, all of which I think is easily solved by 'keeping calm, keeping educated and carrying on'.

The premise for the book is that it's the entrepreneurs not the politicians that will take us though Brexit.

Ultimately, where there is disruption in a market it is the individuals who embrace change that win.

Of course, the referendum laid bare some further divisions in our country, the baby boomers turning out in mass to vote on the future of all other generations.

The millennials who feel that UK politics misunderstands them not voting in sufficient numbers to make up the short fall.

It was also plain to see that many voted as a protest against an undeserving system, feeling they are being left behind, versus those who are prospering who can easily buy their own home, send their children to a great school, and find a secure job.

Those for whom our country works well, and those for whom it does not, put a cross in the same box.

As a business community, we need to leave the politics and any spilt milk at the front door. It is time to direct our energy into our new place in the world.

Let's take up the mantel of the post Brexit Brand Britain and fly the flag globally, for trade, for opportunity, for being human in the way we operate overseas and for putting back into the UK economy.

As an entrepreneur, consider your options and seek out government incentives that suit your business goals, maybe even align them with national goals such as using a grant to build UK based manufacturing plants in areas that are crying out for more opportunities or make the most of the government's apprentice incentives that will see thousands of kids who have been left behind by education get a foot on the ladder and start growing as people.

Work with new technology and be part of the wave transforming every industry. Never get too comfortable doing the same thing year on year, 'disrupt or be disrupted' should become part of your mantra.

Be relentless in your pursuit of success. If you work not just hard, but smart, the pay off in feeling and purpose will be tenfold.

Always stay hungry for information but remember advice is just someone's opinion, you do not have to take it, but you should always listen to it.

If we, the entrepreneurs of this country, pull it off, the result will be a truly united Britain, one that has been united as four nations, united in currency, united in opportunities and united by the principle that it is only your talent and hard work that should determine your success.

We have a golden opportunity to make a success of the disruption in the markets, so that whoever you are, wherever you live, take the bull by the horns and power through Brexit.

The opportunity is global so make the politics, economy, technology and society work for you.

Acknowledgments

Thank you to...

Jane Frankland, Managing Director, Cyber Security Capital (CS^) & Board Advisor, ClubCISO, for your insights on thought leadership

Robin Horsley Independent Brexit Campaigner, Serial Entrepreneur and Founder of Silicon Systems

Zaid Al-Zaidy, chief executive of Marketing agency McCann London

Carmina Lees, Director, Security Business Unit, UK & Ireland for his insights on influencer marketing

Jake Liddell, Digital Marketing Guru

Victoria Christopher, the grammar and spelling queen

Dennis Woods, Dad and Hero

Suzan Woods, Mum and Superwoman

Jenny Woods, Sister, Social Media Royalty

Tim Woods, Brother, Business Partner and rock

Artwork credits:
SWOT Analysis Designed by Freepik

Cover design by pro_design

About The Author

Richard Woods, is an award-winning entrepreneur, BBC's The Apprentice finalist, professional keynote speaker, radio presenter, investor & bestselling author.

He runs a portfolio of businesses including:

- A Digital Marketing Agency - Yomp Marketing

- The UK first Lead Generation Academy – Lead Gen Academy

- A Leading Marketing Events Brand - The Lead Gen Summit

- A Digital Asset Company - Yomp Consultancy

- An Asset Management Business - Woods Capital

- A short-terms letting business – Castle Properties

His first book 'Digital TrailBlazer' went straight to #1 Best Seller on Amazon and continues to sell globally.

He was a finalist upon BBC's The Apprentice, Series 11 (2015) – where he was the top seller across all tasks during the competition. He won 8 out of 10 tasks (second on the all-time list) and broke two Apprentice records one for most sales in one day (£4.3 million) and secondly "The best Advertising Task ever seen on The Apprentice" – Lord Sugar

He has won Young Entrepreneur of the Year 2016 (Haines Watts – Regional Winner), Key Person of Influence Award 2015 (Dent Global Annual Awards), involved in Marketing Campaign of the Year 2015 (Inspire Business Awards).

Richard makes regular appearances on Eagle Radio, BBC Surrey, BBC Asian Network, Marlow FM and BBC Radio 1.

He is a frequent speaker at large business events, trade shows and seminars.

He proudly studied 'Business with Entrepreneurship' at Southampton Solent University and received a first class hons for his final dissertation 'Is there a link between Dyslexia and Entrepreneurship'.

He is 34 years old and based in Surrey, England.

Married to Cara, son Mylo and daughter Poppy.

Next Steps

For Brexitpreneurship resources and events visit:

www.brexitpreneurship.com

Printed in Great Britain
by Amazon